POTAT

AN APPRECIATION

POTATOES

AN APPRECIATION

Judith Millidge

This edition published by Kerswell Books Ltd

Printed 2010

This book is distributed in the UK by
Parkham Books Ltd
Kerswell Farm,
Parkham Ash, Bideford
Devon, England
EX39 5PR

enquiries@parkhambooks.co.uk

ISBN: 978-1-906239-60-2

DS0208. Potatoes - an appreciation

Creative Director: Sarah King
Editor: Clare Haworth-Maden
Project editor: Anna Southgate
Designer: Jade Sienkiewicz

Printed in Singapore

1 3 5 7 9 10 8 6 4 2

CONTENTS

'D'YA WANT FRIES WITH THAT?'

Potatoes are one of the most versatile foodstuffs on the planet. Tough, hardy plants, they will grow in the most unaccommodating of soils and climates, and produce a leafy, beautifully blossomed plant that hides the tuberous spud underneath. The muddy tubers are as unappealing as they are unyielding when they are first dug from the ground, but after a little scrubbing to remove the dirt, and twenty or so minutes in a pan of boiling water, they emerge as a delicious addition to any meal. In fact, they can make a meal in themselves.

Baked, mashed, boiled, and, most popular of all, fried, they sustain millions of people every day of the week. It's slightly depressing that, for many people the world over, fries produced by fast-food joints are their only regular encounter with a potato, because the potato has many different culinary guises. And it seems incredible that a vegetable so rich in nutrients could have been omitted from the list of foods that provide your 'five a day' of fresh produce. Indeed, nutritionists claim that potatoes alone will sustain a healthy adult – although a varied diet is definitely a more interesting prospect for most of us!

Potatoes are grown all over the world, and will thrive in the most difficult of conditions. Originally from South America, for centuries wild potatoes sustained the Indians of the Andes, who managed

One of the earliest botanical illustrations of the potato plant, solanum tuberosum, drawn by the Swiss botanist Gaspard Bauhin in 1591.

to cultivate them in the dry, windswept soil of the mountains. These knobbly little tubers probably bore little relation to the spuds that most of us encounter today, but the potato plant proved to be both hardy and adaptable as it was transplanted from Peru to almost every continent on Earth – and beyond. In 1995, a potato plant was transported into space aboard the Space Shuttle *Columbia* as part of an experiment that investigated the effects of zero gravity on plant growth. The potato plant remained fit and healthy, and maybe one day others will be carried aboard spacecraft on longer interplanetary flights, providing a food source, as well as a means of photosynthesis, within the spacecraft.

On his voyage aboard HMS *Beagle* from 1835 to 1836, the great naturalist Charles Darwin noted many different varieties of wild potatoes around the coast and interior of South America, and in his later years explored ways to create hardy, disease-resistant hybrid potato plants. He was not the first, and will certainly not be the last. From the mid-18th century, growers have worked to produce varieties that will emerge from the ground large, healthy and free from blight and other pests. This remains an on-going job, but there are now well over five thousand different varieties grown around the world, while the potato is the world's fourth-largest food crop after rice, wheat and maize. Farmers have also developed varieties that thrive in their own local conditions and produce as high a yield per acre as possible.

Right: Victims of the Irish potato famine, from the Illustrated London News, 1849.

Below: A 1910 image of one lucky American housewife in her state-of-the-art kitchen, peeling potatoes. (Library of Congress)

All potatoes are descended from two main South American varieties: the Chilean and the Andean. The Chilean potato has adapted itself to grow in the long-day conditions of the area, while the Andean potato thrives in the high-altitude, short-day surroundings of Peru. Genetic variety is critical to the survival of all living things, and the dangers of relying on one particular variety (and, in fact, on one vegetable crop) can be seen in the dreadful aftermath of the 1845–52 potato blight in Ireland. It has been estimated that the failure of the potato crop over two years caused a million deaths from starvation and the emigration of a million and a half more people – not to mention the misery endured by the surviving population. And yet, blight apart, potatoes had sustained the Irish population for a hundred and fifty years, and had proved remarkably useful for peasant farmers wherever they were introduced throughout Europe. High-yielding plants, they require only a small space in which to grow, and, once lifted, the potatoes can be cooked and consumed very quickly and cheaply – unlike cereal crops, which require further processing before consumption. Potatoes are now grown throughout the developing world for exactly these reasons.

POTATO TRIVIA

HERE ARE JUST A FEW FASCINATING FACTS ABOUT POTATOES.

• Slovenia was one of the last countries in Europe to adopt the potato. In fact, the people were forced to grow it by the Archduchess Maria Theresa in 1767, after a series of poor harvests destroyed the grain crop. The arrival of the potato saved the country from starvation and transformed the economy. One town exported so many potatoes to Austria and Germany that it became known as Kartoffeldorf, or 'Potato Village'.

• In Russia, there is still controversy over whether it was Tsar Peter the Great or Catherine the Great who introduced the potato to the country. In 1697, Peter toured western Europe and may well have sent a bag of spuds home. In any case, the potato remained unpopular for much of the 18th century, when it was known as the 'devil's apple' and was believed to be poisonous.

• Potatoes have always been highly valued as a filling, and usually tasty, food. During the 1849 Yukon gold rush in North America, when prospectors headed to shanty towns thrown up in haste and lacking in provisions, potatoes changed hands for gold nuggets – and so were then quite literally worth their weight in gold.

Weather
6 am to midnight

• From the 17th century until the 19th, potatoes were used to cure rheumatism and coughs. Because the plant is a member of the nightshade family (Solanum), medical practitioners believed that it shared some of the nightshades' medicinal properties. According to Nathaniel Chapman, the author of *Elements of Therapeutics and Materia Medica*, published in 1831, the potato had been prescribed 'for protracted coughs – in chronic rheumatism – in *angina pectoris* – in *cephalalgia* – in a case of calculus lodged in the ureter and in cancer of the uterus, in all which diseases it proved highly advantageous'.

• Fish and chips – a combination of flavours made in heaven – helped to sustain British factory workers exhausted after long shifts. By 1910, there were some 25,000 chip shops in Great Britain, with fish and chips enlivening an otherwise dismal and unhealthy working-class diet. People who were too tired to cook could afford a fish-and-chip supper, and, if they added mushy peas as a side dish, were assured of getting a nutritionally balanced meal. Winston Churchill called fish and chips 'the good companions', and they were one of the few foodstuffs to escape rationing during World War II.

• During World War II, Britons were urged to 'Dig for Victory', while Potato Pete was a character dreamt up by the Ministry of Food to educate the public regarding healthy and filling meals. Potatoes were one of the few foodstuffs that were not rationed, and books, posters and even a poem about spuds contributed to the war effort:

'Here's the man who ploughs the fields.
Here's the girl who lifts up the yield.
Here's the man who deals with the clamp,
so that millions of jaws can chew and champ.
That's the story and here's the star,
Potato Pete
Eat up,
Ta-ta!'

• The combination of poor weather in early 1947 and an increased demand arising from the return of demobilised men from wartime armies caused potatoes to be rationed for six months in Britain between 1947 and 1948. The rationing of this staple food was immensely unpopular and prompted considerable questioning from members of the British parliament concerning the supply of potatoes to fish-and-chip shops, soldiers and vegetarians.

• Potato Pete is one of a small élite of popular potato cartoon characters. The Hasbro toy Mr Potato Head is probably the world's most famous toy potato, as well as its only potato film star. (He and his lovely wife, Mrs Potato Head, provided tuberous support in the films *Toy Story* and *Toy Story 2*.) Mr Potato Head was launched in 1952 as a plastic toy with detachable parts that enabled children to make funny faces on the basic potato shape.

Right: Potato harvesters work in Colorado, 1939. The twine carried by the woman is used for sewing up potato sacks. (Library of Congress)

SCHOOL
SCHOOL DAYS POTATO HEAD PENCIL CASE

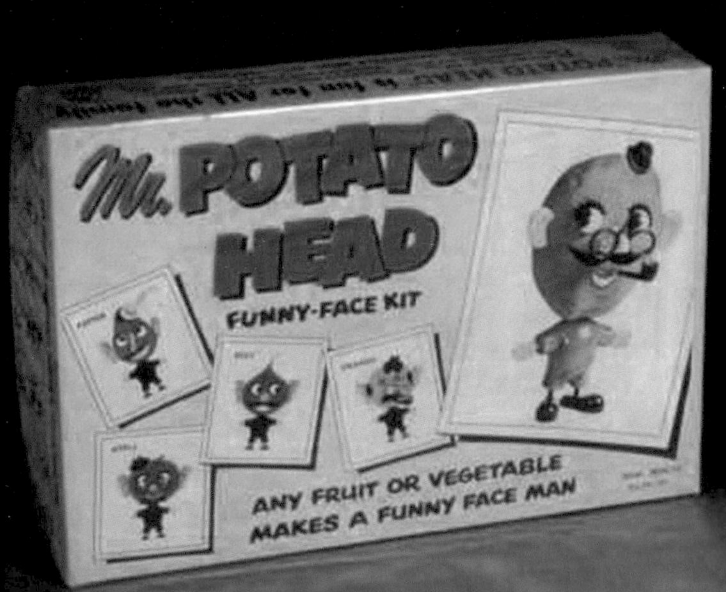
Mr. POTATO HEAD
FUNNY-FACE KIT
ANY FRUIT OR VEGETABLE MAKES A FUNNY FACE MAN

Mr. "POTATO HEAD"
FUNNY FACE IDEAS

Left: Early examples of the popular Mr Potato Head toy.

He was also the first toy to be advertised on television. Mr Potato Head stood for election as mayor in Boise, Idaho, in 1985; he received four votes. Nearly sixty years after his introduction, Mr Potato Head remains an immensely popular toy, and Hasbro has diversified, producing Star Wars-, Indiana Jones- and Spider Man-themed versions.

• In 1974, Eric Jenkins grew 168 kg of potatoes from a single plant in England – a world record that still stands today. The following year, the largest potato grown in England weighed an impressive 8 kg.

• In 2008, the United Nations declared that that year would be the International Year of the Potato in recognition of the huge importance of potatoes in the diet of people in the developing world, as well as in Western nations. The International Potato Center (CIP) in Lima, Peru – Peru being the birthplace of the potato – was at the heart of the celebrations and events intended to raise the profile of potatoes. (Over five thousand varieties of a hundred wild-potato species are maintained by the CIP to preserve the biodiversity of the plant and ensure that there is a continuous supply of new varieties.)

WHOLESOME AND DELICIOUS VEGETABLES

The potato is such a central part of the Western diet that we could be forgiven for thinking that it has been grown in northern Europe forever.

Roast beef, Yorkshire pudding and roast potatoes; fish and chips; sausage and mash – these are the nearest that the British have to national dishes, and all of them are Victorian in origin. It seems a shame to shatter the illusion, but while we're at it, Sir Walter Raleigh probably did not bring back potatoes from his short-lived colony in North America and cook them for Queen Elizabeth I – before offering her a post-prandial pipe stuffed with his new supply of tobacco leaves. Sir Francis Drake may have brought some potato plants back from Peru (via raids on the Spanish treasure fleet in the Caribbean) in 1573, but it is most likely that potatoes arrived in England through trade with European neighbours. Potatoes were certainly known in Elizabethan England, but they were not widely cultivated until the 18th century.

Right: A copy of the 'Gloriana' portrait of Elizabeth I. Her patronage of explorers such as Raleigh and Drake helped to establish the potato in Europe.

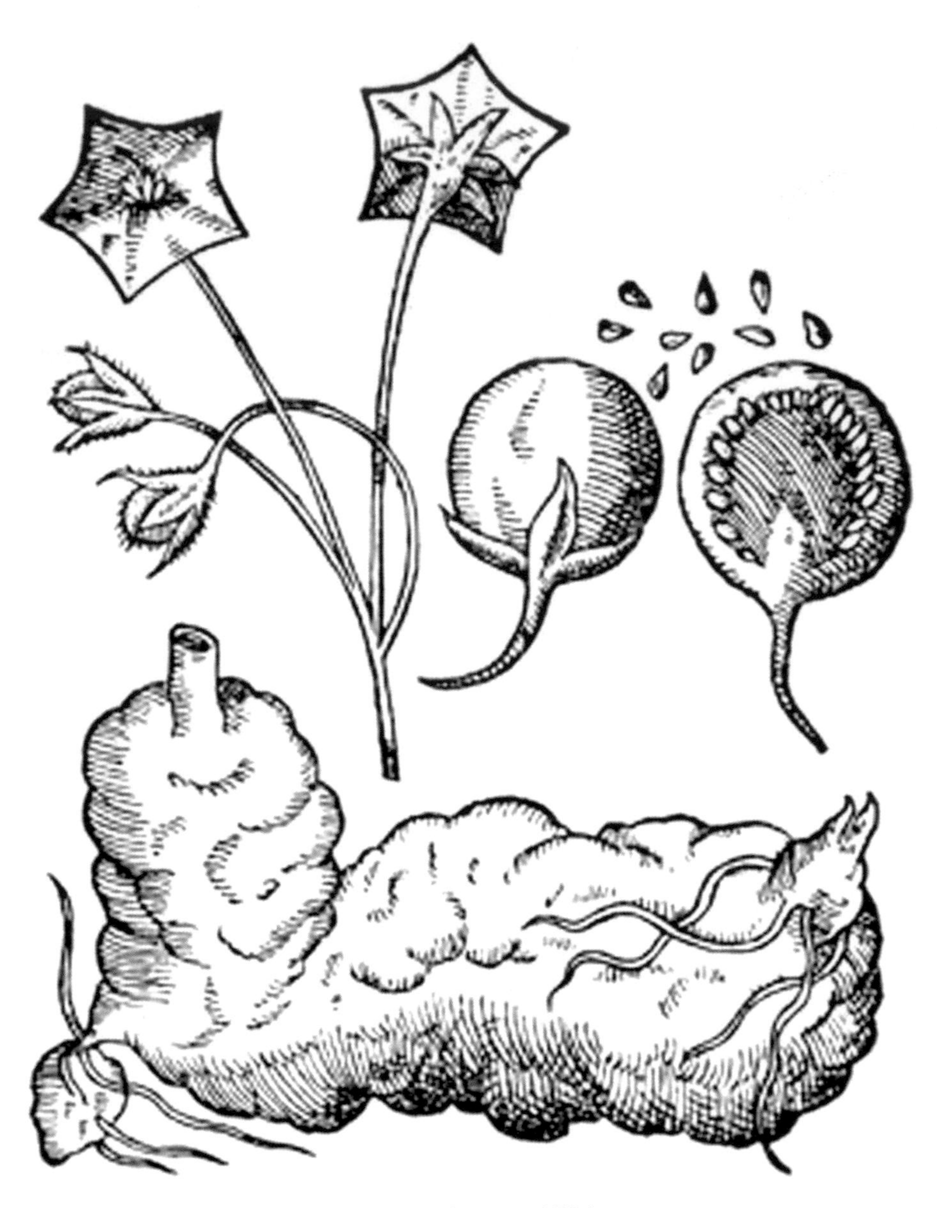

Solanum tuberosum bt Gaspard Bauhin, 1591.

The word 'potato' is derived from the Spanish *batata* and the Quechan (the language of the Incas) word papa, and for several decades in 16th-century Europe potatoes were confused with sweet potatoes, although the vegetables are not related. The potato, or *Solanum tuberosum*, has been grown in the Andes for thousands of years, and was spread around the world by the Spanish explorers of the 16th century. When they explored the South American continent from 1524, the Spanish were not terribly interested in the diet of the native peoples. Led by the great conquistador Francisco Pizarro, they were overwhelmed by the sight of silver, gold, precious stones and strange new creatures, such as llamas. And they also had to deal with the hostility of the Incas, so small, brown, egg-shaped tubers buried under leafy plants were not the first items that grabbed their attention. The Spanish brought with them provisions and supplies intended to replicate the Spanish way of life in the New World, and it was really only in extremis, when hardship and hunger overcame them, that they were forced to emulate the natives and eat their food. So the potato was initially regarded as a peasant foodstuff fit only for the godless Indians, and therefore not worthy of attention.

'Bread of the Indians'

Despite their initial misgivings, natural curiosity combined with hunger ensured that the Spanish not only came to eat potatoes within a few years of their arrival in South America, but also sent some back to Spain. And when confronted with the staple food of Peru, the Spanish chroniclers generally praised the potato: Juan de Castellanos, writing as early as 1536, said, 'It is a gift very acceptable to the Indians, and a dainty dish even for the Spaniards'. In 1590, José de Acosta noted that there was a substantial trade in *chuño* (local dried potato), which was used to feed the enslaved workers of the silver mines at Potosí, in Bolivia. Indeed, a few Spaniards made their fortunes selling *chuño*, rather than acquiring silver.

During the 17th century, in his *Historia del Nuevo Mundo* (*History of the New World*), the Jesuit priest Bernabé Cobo (who spent most of his life in South America) referred to the potato as 'the bread of the Indians', which sums up its importance as a staple food in the Andes. So central to daily life in pre-Columbian South America was the potato that it determined measurement systems: measuring the passage of time was based on how long it took to boil a pot of potatoes, while the basic measurement of land was fixed on the size of a plot needed to grow enough potatoes to feed a family. The Andean people also developed methods for preserving potatoes to ensure a year-long supply. The climate of the mountains is dry, with a wide range of temperatures, from freezing nights

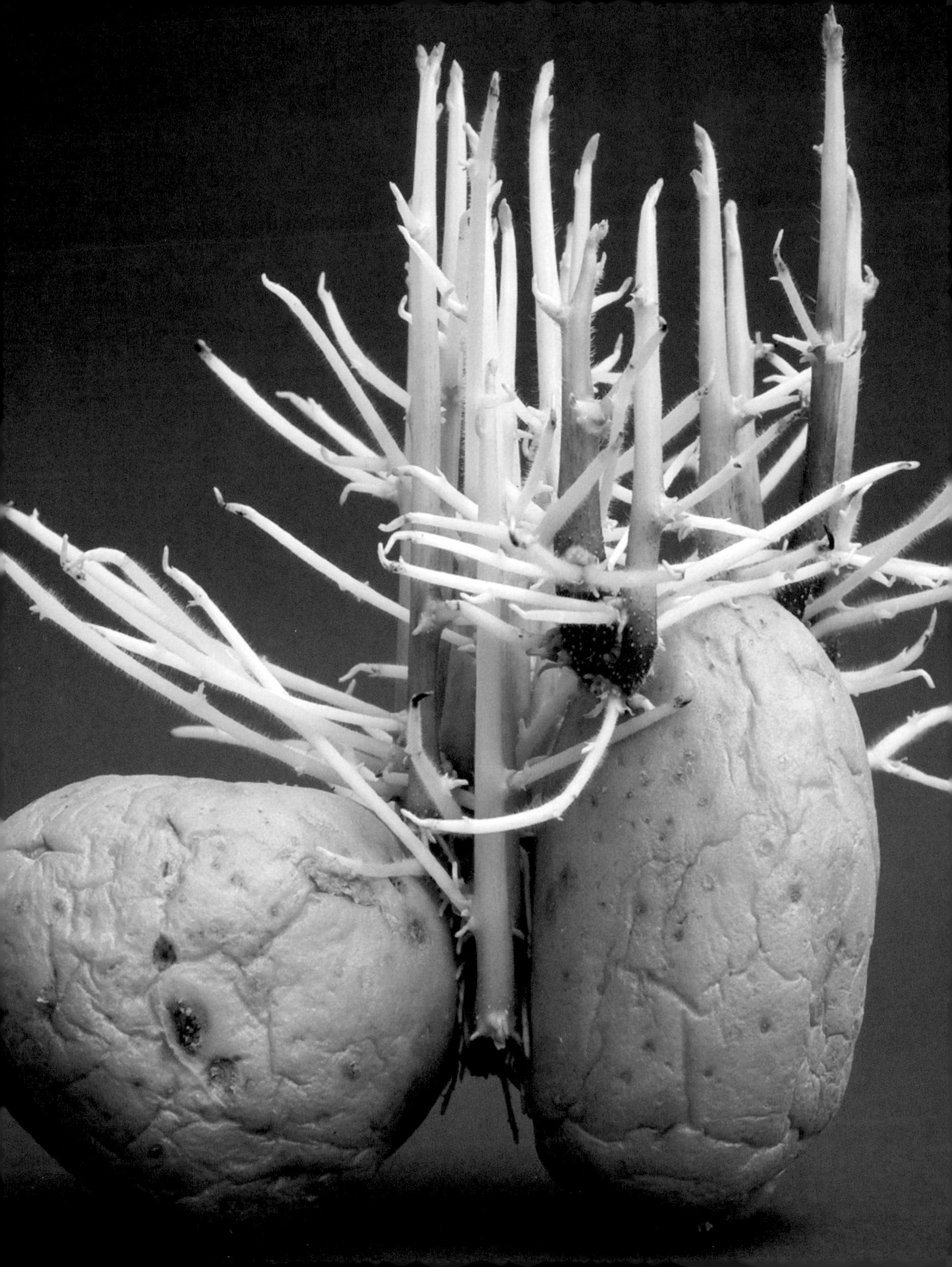

to temperate days. When the potatoes were harvested, they were left outside to freeze for several nights, and were then placed in water for about a month. At the end of the month, the tubers were scattered on the ground and trodden underfoot to squeeze out the water and remove the skins. The remaining potato pulp was left outside for two more weeks to dehydrate in the sun and freeze at night. What was left was called *chuño*, and this could be stored for years without rotting. This ancient process – possibly dating back over two thousand years – sustained the people of the Andes for generations.

Not surprisingly, the potato plant plays an important role in the myths and legends of the Andean people. Artefacts from the Moche civilisation (AD100–600), which is far older than that of the Incans, show human and animal figures sprouting from the potato's eyes; the potato was clearly at the centre of their creation myth. Peruvian folk religion still reveres unusually shaped tubers as a sign of fertility and a good harvest. The Spanish priest Francisco de Avila (1573–1647) recorded a great many traditional Indian rites and customs, including the myth about the god Huatya Curi, in his treatise *Errors, False Gods, and Other Superstitions of the Indians of the Provinces of Huarochiri, Mama, and Chaclla* in 1608. Huatya Curi, originally a poor man, is the embodiment of the potato: his lowly, dirty appearance hides his talents, which he uses to good effect to triumph over his wicked, richer brother-in-law.

'A pernicious substance'

Potatoes seem to have taken a slightly circuitous route from Peru to mainland Europe. Although many surviving Spanish documents record exactly what was loaded aboard Spanish treasure ships in terms of bullion and artefacts, there is little about plants. It seems likely that potatoes crossed the Atlantic almost by accident. Many plants from the New World arrived first in the Canary Islands, where the warm climate was conducive to experimentation and propagation, and their fruits or seeds were then sent on to mainland Spain. Fragments of shipping records suggest that potatoes had arrived in the Canaries by 1562, thirty years after the Spanish conquest of Peru. And barrels of potatoes were certainly being sent to northern Europe by the late 1560s. It also seems likely that potatoes were sent around the world either deliberately, or almost by accident, as the tubers self-propagated in dark nooks and crannies and were then planted out. Accounting records from the Spanish city of Seville show that potatoes were on sale there as early as 1573, and that their price became lower as the decade wore on, this was presumably because their cultivation became more widespread.

PAPAS COLO
O
COLORADAS
(Solanum tuberosum
El primer puerto europeo al qu
Andes en a Canarias. Adapt
islas, las papas de colo
calidad y completame
comunes en

During the 16th century, Spanish explorers and traders took potato plants around the world, to the Far East, as well as to Europe. Potato plants had spread from the Spanish Philippines to China, Japan and India by the late 17th century. In 1621, the governor of Bermuda sent a crop of potatoes to Francis Wyatt, governor of the colony of Virginia, and this is certainly the first-recorded instance of the arrival of potatoes in North America. In 1640, English immigrants introduced potatoes to County Wicklow in Ireland, but during the 17th century, they were used more often as feed for livestock than as a supplement to the human diet.

What is truly remarkable about the potato is that, unlike many plants that are planted, nurtured, produce edible fruits or useful seeds and then die, potatoes regenerate themselves. Under the right conditions, a potato will produce shoots or chits, and, if planted in the ground, will generate many more tubers. Something of a botanical curiosity, when they became more commonplace during the later 16th century, potatoes were regarded with suspicion, partly because they were tubers that emerged from the soil, which was considered the domain of the Devil. The plants themselves resembled several others: their stems looked like those of tomato plants, while their berries were similar to those of mandrake plants, and worse still, the deadly nightshade. By 1596, the Swiss botanist Gaspard Bauhin had classified the potato as *Solanum tuberosum*, a member of the Solanaceae, or nightshade, family. And with relatives that included plants used to make poisons, potions and medicinal draughts, the potato acquired an unjustified reputation as a dangerous root vegetable.

Right: The Elizabethan herbalist John Gerard, from the frontispiece of his 1597 book, Great Herball, or Generall Historie of Plantes. He is holding a potato plant.

The English herbalist and doctor, John Gerard (1545–1612), who supervised the gardens of Lord Burghley, Elizabeth I's senior minister, produced the first illustration of a potato plant in his *Herball* of 1597. Gerard grew potatoes in his London garden and says that he 'received rootes hereof from Virginia which grow and prosper as in their native country'. The well-connected Gerard, himself a former ship's doctor, may have known Sir Walter Raleigh and Sir Francis Drake (who had been bothering the Spanish treasure fleets in the Caribbean), and it is not impossible that a member of Raleigh's expedition gave Gerard some tubers on his return from the first, ill-fated English colonies founded on Roanoake Island during the 1580s. Gerard is known to have plagiarised much of his book, but there was no earlier botanical source that included *Solanum tuberosum*, and for all of its faults, the *Herball's* description of the potato is an original one. Indeed, Gerard was so taken with it that the frontispiece of the book depicts the author holding a potato flower.

In Britain, potatoes were initially regarded as something of a delicacy. In 1619, the queen's household purchased a small quantity of potatoes for the extremely high price of a shilling per pound. In 1662, a Somerset farmer, a Mr Buckland, recommended to the Royal Society the planting of potatoes throughout the country to prevent famine, and once its learned members had examined his proposal, they recommended that all members who had land should follow his advice.

London Printed by
Adam Islip Joice Norton
and Richard Whitakers
Anno 1636.

By 1650, the potato was known throughout Europe, but it was certainly not embraced as a useful new food crop. The French thought that it caused leprosy, and an edict in the town of Besançon in 1630 banned its cultivation: 'In view of the fact that the potato is a pernicious substance whose use can cause leprosy, it is hereby forbidden, under pain of fine, to cultivate it'. As late as the 18th century, a few clergymen were discouraging their flocks from planting potatoes in their gardens because they were not mentioned in the Bible. However, potatoes gradually infiltrated the European diet and became a useful supplement to a diet that depended on cereal crops.

'A plant so innocent . . .'

It took the vast changes wrought by population growth and the Industrial Revolution to turn the potato into a staple food. Unlike cereal crops, potato plants can be easily grown in gardens or on smallholdings, and the food that they produce needs no further refinement: potatoes can be put straight into a cooking pot and can then be cooked and eaten within half an hour of being harvested. (Cereal crops, of course, need milling and grinding before they can be used.) So as growing numbers of people moved from the countryside to towns, householders came to appreciate the potato as a useful supplement to their diet. In many ways, potatoes were the first fast food of the industrial age. The new urban poor, who worked long hours and then returned

Left: Potato harvester at work in the Midwest in 1909.
(Library of Congress)

home to generally squalid conditions, generally lacked either the energy or the means to do much cooking. Potatoes were cheap to purchase (if they could not be grown at home), required little fuel to cook and provided a filling and reasonably nutritious meal. By the late 18th century, British statesman Edmund Burke was describing the potato as 'A plant so innocent, so agreeable and so productive'.

At the turn of the 18th and 19th centuries, a number of writers who commented on the changes in rural England and the growth of urban living caused by the Industrial Revolution were noting that potatoes were grown everywhere, from farms to small urban gardens. William Cobbett, the journalist and reformer, toured the country and recounted his experiences in his book *Rural Rides*. He was dismissive of potatoes, but such contemporaries as Arthur Young, later first secretary at the Board of Agriculture, recognised their value. In 1776, Young saw for himself that potatoes were being grown across Britain, from Wiltshire to west Wales, reporting: 'The culture of potatoes increases much, more planted last year than ever known before. The poor eat them: and every cabbin has a garden with some in it'. Historians now believe that the potato was such a valuable foodstuff that it helped to account for the 65 per cent increase in Europe's population from 1700.

Right: A copy of The Potato Harvest by Jules Breton.
(Library of Congress)

Crop failures during the 18th century also increased the potato's popularity as people were driven to eat them out of necessity. In 1771, the French government asked the Faculty of Medicine in Paris to provide a scientific assessment of potatoes, and it pronounced them to be wholesome, useful food.

There are several instances throughout Europe of towns of starving citizens rejecting cartloads of potatoes because they perceived them as being harmful. In 1774, Frederick the Great of Prussia sent free potatoes to starving peasants in Kolberg, but they were deeply suspicious of them and refused to eat them, saying, 'The things have neither smell nor taste, not even the dogs will eat them, so what use are they to us?' A Swabian soldier was dispatched to the town to persuade the people of the potatoes' virtues and to show them how to plant, grow and cook them. The War of the Bavarian Succession, which occurred a few years later (1778–79), was a conflict defined more by the time that the Austrian and Prussian troops spent scavenging for food and denying supplies to the enemy, which is why it became known as the 'Potato War'.

In Sweden, the great naturalist Carl Linnaeus encouraged the planting of potatoes, but it was not until a royal edict of 1764 enforced their cultivation that they were more widely grown. The botanist Henry Philips noted that the Swedish used them to distil brandy 'in order to save corn, which in that country is often very dear'. He repeated the recipe: 72 lb (32.7 kg) of potatoes produced a gallon (3.8 l) of pure spirit, 'the finest and most agreeably vinous spirit . . . ever tasted'. Potatoes continued to be something of a niche crop in parts of Europe, however. It took two key interventions to make the potato more widely accepted during the late 18th century: the hard work of one dedicated agriculturalist and the glamour of celebrity.

Right: During the 19th century potato varieties were dispersed across the USA and Europe by keen, largely amateur, horticulturalists.

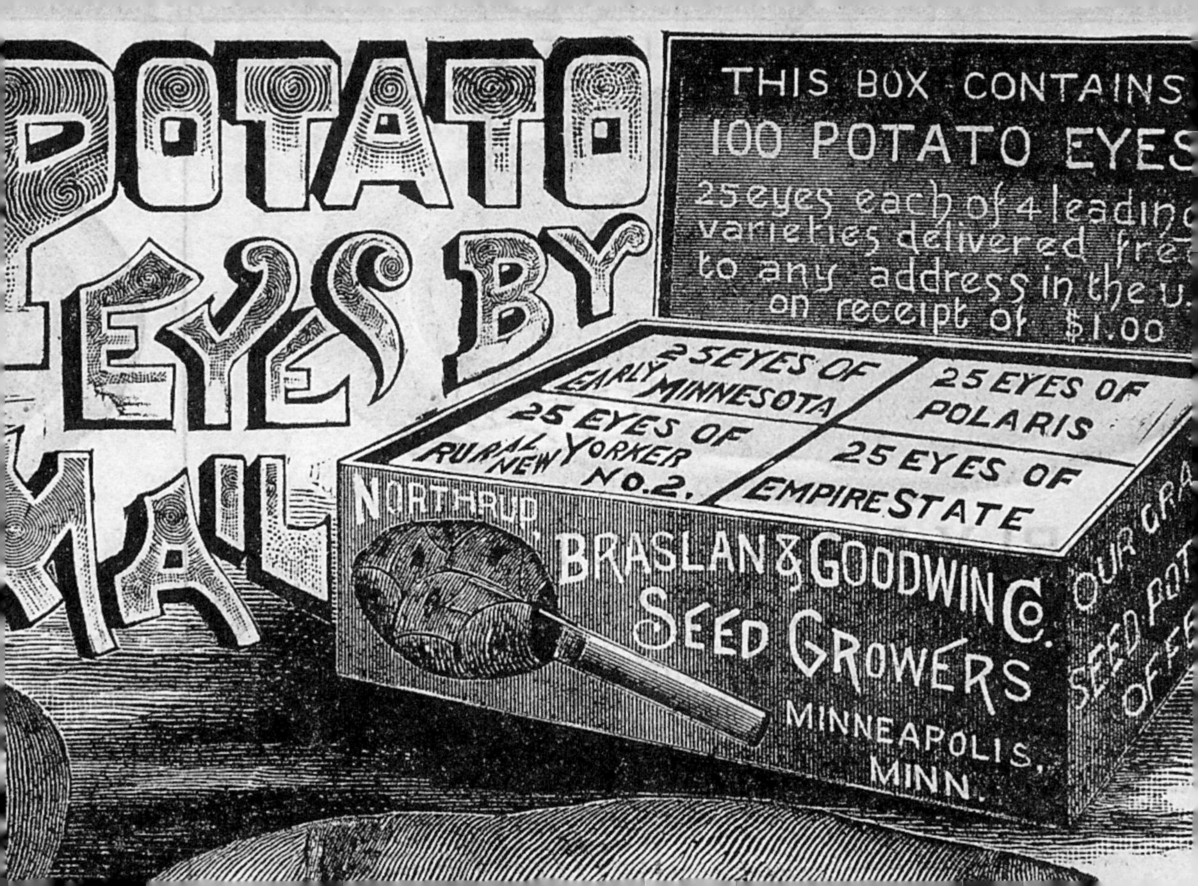
POTATO EYES BY MAIL
THIS BOX CONTAINS
100 POTATO EYES
25 eyes each of 4 leading
varieties delivered free
to any address in the U.
on receipt of $1.00
25 EYES OF
EARLY MINNESOTA
25 EYES OF
POLARIS
25 EYES OF
RURAL NEW YORKER
No. 2.
25 EYES OF
EMPIRE STATE
NORTHRUP,
BRASLAN & GOODWIN CO.
SEED GROWERS
MINNEAPOLIS,
MINN.

Parmentier's 'bread for the poor'

Antoine-Augustin Parmentier (1737–1813) was a great intellectual force of the Enlightenment, a man who worked to convince those around him of the usefulness of his beliefs. A pharmacist by training, he served with the French Army during the Seven Years' War (1756–63) and was captured by the Prussians. The French prisoners were treated to a diet consisting almost entirely of potatoes, which the French utterly despised, as potatoes were used as animal feed within France. Despite their disgust, the prisoners thrived, and when Parmentier returned to Paris in 1763 (in rude health) he continued his researches into nutritional chemistry. He was largely responsible for persuading the Paris Faculty of Medicine to declare, in 1771, that potatoes were not only edible, but also actually useful as a staple food. During the early 1770s, food prices and shortages were constant concerns in France, and Parmentier realised that potatoes could solve the problems of supply if only he could overcome the French prejudice against them.

Something of a showman, in 1785, Parmentier presented the French king and queen, Louis XVI and Marie Antoinette (left), with gifts of potato flowers to wear as buttonholes, and with potatoes on the menu at the king's birthday party, the rest of the aristocracy rushed to copy their royal masters. Potatoes became fashionable!

Realising that potatoes would only be widely cultivated if landowners were on his side, Parmentier organised a series of dinners in Paris, to which he invited the celebrities of the day: influential people, such as the then American ambassador to France, Benjamin Franklin; the chemist Antoine Lavoisier; and the French king and queen. His guests were treated to twenty courses of potato dishes, each one served differently.

Parmentier used a little low cunning to persuade France's poor citizens of the benefits of potatoes. In 1787, he planted a field of potatoes outside Paris, which he was careful to guard during the day. At night, it was widely known that the guards stood down, allowing local peasants to sneak in and steal the potatoes. Parmentier, of course, did nothing to stop them – somehow contraband potatoes tasted better than those forced on the poor by well-meaning benefactors.

One of the causes of the French Revolution was the price of bread, which had risen sharply after several years of poor grain harvests. By 1795, during the siege of the Paris Commune, potatoes were being grown in the gardens of the Tuileries Palace to combat the widespread starvation caused by the siege.

Parmentier died in 1813, having rendered an extraordinary service to France during a very difficult period. His name lives on today in a number of potato recipes, such as pommes Parmentier, and in a station on the métro, the underground railway system in Paris. A statue in his native town of Montdidier depicts the great man handing out seed potatoes to grateful peasants, who had finally been convinced of the potato's usefulness.

General O'Hara taken prisoner at the siege of Toulon.

Parmentier's insistence that potatoes were a useful supplement to the human diet helped alleviate food shortages in Revolutionary France.

'A fatal malady has broken out among the potato crop ...'

In Ireland, unlike in France, the general population needed no encouragement to grow potatoes. The potato had been introduced to Ireland during the 17th century, simply as an addition to the gentleman landlord's garden. Very quickly, however, cultivation increased as people realised that the potato was a valuable additional food crop. Cheap to grow and easy to harvest, potatoes seemed ideally suited to the conditions of Irish agriculture, and by the early 18th century they had become a mainstay of the peasants' diet.

By the end of the century, economists had realised that the potato was responsible for sustaining the Irish labour force. Adam Smith wrote, in *The Wealth of Nations*, that if potatoes occupied 'the same proportion of the lands in tillage which wheat and other sorts of grain for human food do at present, the same quantity of cultivated land would maintain a much greater number of people'. He was right, but he did not foresee the dangers of an entire population depending on one crop for its main source of food. The more pessimistic Thomas Malthus was little more realistic, writing in 1826 that if the potato crop failed, it would leave the people who depended on it 'absolutely without resource'. Twenty years later, between 1845 and 1852, this is exactly what happened, and the population of Ireland, left 'without resource', starved. Many of those who survived emigrated.

The population declined by a quarter: a million people died, and a further million left the country. The 1842 census showed that the population of Ireland then stood at 8 million people, and that two-thirds of the workforce depended on agriculture for their living. With wages low, people worked for landlords in return for a patch of land, which they used to grow crops to support their families. The potato supplied abundant food in return for minimal effort, but, like all crops, was susceptible to disease and pests. The potato harvest failed several times during the 18th century, and fourteen times between 1800 and 1840. It was the arrival of potato blight in 1845 that caused utter devastation, destroying the potato harvest and causing large numbers of a population already weakened by subsistence living to die.

Potato blight, or *Phytophthora infestans (right)*, thrives in mild, wet conditions and can be spread from plant to plant on the wind. Initially visible as brown marks on the leaves of the plant, the disease causes a potato plant to curl up and die. Even worse, spores may be washed into the soil, where they remain to infect the next crop. The disease originated in Mexico during the 1840s and was borne by the wind to the north-eastern United States. It is thought that it crossed the Atlantic in 1844, on a shipment of seed potatoes destined for Belgium. Potato blight also had a devastating effect on parts of northern Europe, including Belgium, the Netherlands, northern France and Germany.

In England, reports of the disease in the *Gardeners' Chronicle and Horticultural Gazette* became increasingly worried, one noting in August 1844 that 'A fatal malady has broken out among the potato crop . . .' The British government was extremely slow to respond to the crisis, and its inaction did little to alleviate the appalling conditions that the Irish were enduring. The Great Famine in Ireland was the catalyst for political upheaval at Westminster as the government was eventually

Henry Mayhew, the London journalist, playwright and keen advocate of social reform (1812-1887).

forced to change not only its trading policies, but also its attitude to Ireland. More importantly, the famine changed Ireland forever, altering its demography, charging relations between the British and Irish with bitterness and agitating the Irish population's nationalist movement.

In 1851, the London journalist Henry Mayhew published his great work, *London Labour and the London Poor*, in which he included his interviews with several baked-potato sellers, noting that they had really only been in evidence for about fifteen years. Hawking baked potatoes was seasonal, but profitable, work for the three hundred or so sellers, but interestingly, one seller noted that trade had recently fallen off: 'People looks very shy at my taties, very', he said. 'They've been more suspicious ever since the taty rot. I thought I should never have rekivered it.'

'Potatoes served at breakfast . . .'

Over the course of the 19th century, as populations spread out across North America, and as the British Empire extended its influence across a quarter of the world's surface, the consumption of the potato increased, too. Gradually, it became a foodstuff that people actually looked forward to eating, rather than being regarded as the food of the desperate. Potatoes were now being readily consumed at every level of society, from the London workers who purchased them for a halfpenny from the baked-potato man to Queen Victoria herself, who let it be known that the Victoria potato was served at the dining tables of Balmoral and Windsor. The middle classes were being well served by the cookery writer Mrs Beeton's recommendations for what she called 'this wholesome and delicious vegetable', which included recipes for boiling, baking and roasting potatoes, as well as the slightly more exotic potato pudding, and instructions on making good use of potato starch.

Despite the USA's geographical proximity to South America, the first potato patch was not planted in North America until 1719. However, with the expansion of the population during the 19th century, and the inexorable move to lands west of the Mississippi River, the potato came to be planted across the continent. And as settlers and immigrants to the USA travelled west across the American prairies, they took with them a wide selection of potatoes, often from their home countries. When they settled on their 160-acre tracts of homestead land, potatoes were often planted first, before any other crops, simply because they yielded food more immediately. The pioneer lifestyle was harsh and generally basic: families often lived in one-roomed cabins, and there was often no space (or, indeed, money) for any kind of oven. So all the cooking was done over an open fire, and potatoes, ever versatile, were highly valued by hungry families. Nutritious and filling, they were ideal food for agricultural labourers and their families – at every meal. As the population settled, the acreage of potato cultivation increased, notably in the northern states, the Midwest and California. A Pennsylvanian prayer ran: 'Potatoes served at breakfast, At dinner served again; Potatoes served at supper, Forever and Amen!'

As the commercial growth of potatoes became big business in the 20th century, particularly in the American midwest, whole communities came to rely on potatoes for their livelihoods. This poster advertises the annual potato barrel rolling contest in a Maine town in 1959 - a popular event with a cash prize of $150. (Library of Congress)

Visitors to the USA were often astonished by the size of the breakfasts there, which may have included pork steaks, potatoes, biscuits, toast, porridge and coffee. The almost accidental invention of potato chips in 1853 coincided with the refinement and mass production of cooking oils, so fried potatoes became increasingly popular. In the cities, tenement living meant that many people, like their country cousins, had no access to a stove, and depended on food that was easy to cook. The same was true in urban areas throughout Europe at the turn of the 19th century.

Potato-breeding

Potato varieties had altered little in the three hundred years since the plant's introduction to Europe, and the blight that caused the Great Famine in Ireland forced potato-growers around the world to develop many more varieties with increased resistance to disease.

Although blight subsequently never destroyed the whole potato crop as it had during the 1840s, localised outbreaks encouraged horticulturists to experiment with developing new varieties that would be less vulnerable to disease. Farmers invested large sums of money in planting different varieties next to each other, to be cross-pollinated by bees in an attempt to raise new varieties that would be blight-resistant and free from pests. In Dundee, William Paterson developed the great Victoria variety between 1856 and 1863, which in its turn was later used as a valuable cross-breeder.

In 1872, in the USA, the amateur botanist Luther Burbank noticed a rare seed berry in his mother's potato plot in Massachusetts. He germinated the seeds from the Early Rose potatoes and developed the highly successful Russet-Burbank, the potato now better known as the Idaho that is still the backbone of the American potato crop. An excellent baker and fryer, it is a staple of the fast-food trade and still accounts for over 40 per cent of American potato production.

As horticulturists and scientists increased their understanding of hereditary principles throughout the 19th century, so the art of growing bigger, and hardier, potatoes became a science with a valuable economic outcome. As populations grew the world over, agriculture adapted to meet the increasing food demands of industrialised societies. Farming gradually became mechanised, and tens of thousands of acres were given over to potato cultivation. Scotland, the Netherlands and Soviet Russia led the world in potato-breeding during the 20th century, and in the early years of the 21st century, developing countries began adopting potatoes as a valuable crop.

S AND H

Potato production and consumption today

Potatoes are now grown in over 130 countries, and are eaten by more than 1 billion people, of every socio-economic group, around the world every year. The people of Belarus eat more than anyone else, consuming 181 kg every year, while the British eat 102 kg per person per year (2005 figures). Although potatoes are supplements to a varied diet in the Western world, they form a vital part of the diet in developing nations. The potato continues to nourish the poor, as it has done for over three hundred years. It is such an adaptable plant that it will grow successfully almost anywhere. Farmers in the tropics can harvest their spuds after just fifty days of cultivation, while growers in more northerly climes must wait for three times as long – but the potato crop is a reliable source of sustenance, so it is worth the wait.

The United Nations named 2008 the 'International Year of the Potato' in order to raise the profile of this very valuable crop. As the world's population increases, so the potato will become even more important as a carbohydrate source in the diets of millions of people in developing nations. As poor Europeans discovered during the 18th century, the potato yields more nourishing food faster, and on a smaller acreage of land, in extreme climates than any other major crop. So in a world where pressure on the basic resources of water and land is increasing every year, the potato, which surrenders 85 per cent of its growth to human consumption, will become increasingly valuable. Potatoes yield more food per unit of water than any other food crop, and are up to seven times more efficient in using water than cereal crops. Potatoes are already the third most important food crop in the world, while potato cultivation has increased more than that of any other major crop in the developing world during the past forty years.

The top ten potato-producing countries in 2007 (according to CIP, the International Potato Center)

Country	Metric tonnes
China	73,461,500
Russian Federation	37,279,820
India	25,000,000
Ukraine	19,462,400
United States	19,097,500
Germany	11,624,000
Poland	10,369,000
Belarus	8,185,010
Netherlands	6,777,000
France	6,680,820

A horse-drawn digger harvests potatoes in 1940, USA. (Library of Congress)

Although production has declined in European countries, potato cultivation in Africa, Asia and Latin America has increased, and this reflects the potato's new importance as a food source in the developing world. A third of the world's potatoes are harvested in China and India.

Britain is the eleventh-largest potato-producing country. In Australia, potatoes are the country's largest vegetable crop, accounting for 17.4 per cent of total vegetable production. Most are grown in the southern states of Tasmania, Victoria and South Australia, and per capita consumption is about 62 kg per year.

A wartime picture comparing three different forms of potato – dehydrated, natural and sliced. It showed how dehydrated potato was the preferred form for shipping around the world to feed the US armed forces. (Library of Congress)

About 50 per cent of the world's potato harvest is eaten fresh. The remainder is used to manufacture processed potato products, such as oven chips, is turned into animal feed, or is processed into starch for industrial purposes. About 10 per cent of the crop is used to provide seed potatoes for the following year. In the USA, most of the country's crop is grown in Idaho, Wisconsin, Washington, North Dakota, Colorado, Oregon, Maine, Minnesota, California and Michigan. Most of the crop – 60 per cent – is processed into frozen, dehydrated or crisp potato products, with only a third of the crop being consumed as fresh potatoes.

POTATO VARIETIES

Potatoes vary in the length of time that they take to mature, and the weather and local soil conditions also play an important part in the process. If you are intending to cultivate potatoes, when choosing what you want to grow, think about the size of your plot, whether you want a small haul of spuds to eat throughout the summer, or whether you would like to store your crop through the winter. Potatoes are divided into four main categories – first and second earlies, and early and late maincrop potatoes – which are defined by when they are ready for harvesting. First and second earlies are usually smaller, and their plants have lower yields, than their maincrop cousins.

• First earlies, more commonly called new potatoes, are planted between January and March and are harvested between May and July, having matured within 60 to 110 days of planting. Jersey Royals are probably the most popular and flavoursome examples. First earlies are usually sold and eaten as soon as they are harvested.

• Second earlies are planted between February and May and take between 110 and 120 days to mature. They are generally ready 13 weeks after planting, between July and October.

• Early maincrop potatoes are planted between March and May, and are ready 125 to 140 days (15 or so weeks) later, from August. Desiree, King Edward and Romano are the best examples.

• Late maincrop potatoes are harvested from September onwards, some 20 weeks after planting.

Gardeners will, however, find that harvesting potatoes is not an exact science, and that much depends on the soil conditions, the weather and the horticultural care of their potato plants.

Different flavours

Potato plants were carried around the world by sailors and explorers, who cultivated them as valuable antidotes to scurvy, and often – possibly inadvertently – planted them on foreign shores. During his five-year voyage aboard HMS *Beagle* from 1831, Charles Darwin stopped off in Australia and New Zealand, where the natural life of the Antipodes amazed him. He recorded the details of his journeys in his journal, noting, among many other things, that the colonists traded potatoes for other useful items, such as whale oil and flax. In 1835, he travelled to New Zealand, writing that, 'The introduction of the potato has been the most essential benefit to the island; it is now much more used than any native vegetable'. In South America, he investigated the diet of the native peoples and was particularly interested in the wild potatoes that he found growing near the shore. Darwin knew that potatoes originated in South America: 'The tubers were generally small, but I found one, of an oval shape, two inches in diameter: they resembled in every respect, and had the same smell as English potatoes; but when boiled they shrunk much, and were watery and insipid, without any bitter taste'. Given the vast difference in climate across the South American continent, he found it remarkable that potatoes could grow in such widely different conditions, from the arid mountains of the Andes to the damp forests of the south. He realised that there were several varieties of potatoes, which had adapted to suit their surroundings. In fact, there are two major subspecies of *Solanum tuberosum*: the Andean potato (*Solanum tuberosum andigena*), which originated in the Andes and is adapted to growing in the short-day conditions of the region, and the Chilean potato (*Solanum tuberosum tuberosum*), which is adapted to the long-day conditions of southern Chile.

There are around 450 varieties of potatoes grown in Great Britain. Many of them are well-

established 'heritage' varieties, while others have been bred more recently to produce the magic combination of a high yield and resistance to disease. Experts generally believe that the older varieties produce more flavoursome potatoes, but agricultural growers who are producing crops for supermarkets need to adapt to the demands of the market, viz., supplying uniform potatoes without spots, eyes or bruises.

There are three main types of potatoes: waxy, firm and floury.

- Waxy potatoes, such as the Charlotte, have a slightly translucent skin and a moist feel. They have a higher water content and a milder flavour than more floury spuds. They are less likely to disintegrate while boiling.

- Firm potatoes, which are useful for slicing and boiling whole, include Desiree, Romano and Pentland Javelin.

- Floury potatoes often have slightly flakier skins and are starchier as they contain less water than waxy potatoes. They are excellent for mashing and make really tasty roast potatoes and chips. Some of the best include King Edward potatoes.

ACCORD

(top right) Accord is a disease-resistant, high-yielding potato that was first bred in 1996. Suitable for short-term storage, it has creamy flesh and a distinctive flavour.

Origin: the Netherlands

Plant: January to March

Harvest: first early, May to June

Type: waxy

Recipe hint: potato wedges

ANYA

(bottom right) A specialist variety with a long, oval body shape, Anya has a nutty taste and is excellent in salads. It is derived from a cross between a Desiree and a Pink Fir Apple.

Origin: Scotland, 1995

Plant: February to May

Harvest: second early, July to August

Type: floury

Recipe hint: salad potatoes

BELLE DE FONTENAY

(top left) With a firm texture and waxy skin, Belle de Fontenay is a venerable salad potato. Its excellent flavour and versatility – it can be eaten with or without its skin, either hot or cold – has made it a classic of French cuisine.

Origin: France, 1885

Plant: March to May

Harvest: maincrop, July to October

Type: waxy

Recipe hint: salad potatoes

CARA

(bottom left) A tough, white potato, with a moist, waxy skin, mild flavour and distinctive pink eyes, Cara is an excellent garden and allotment spud. It produces abundant yields and repels pests and diseases with great vigour.

Origin: Ireland, 1976

Plant: March to May

Harvest: maincrop, July to October

Type: waxy

Recipe hint: jacket potatoes

CARLINGFORD

(top right) Carlingford is a firm potato with a white skin and white flesh; it is usually round and smooth. Similar to the Maris Piper (see page 90), it can be planted late for a second crop of new potatoes at the year's end.

Origin: Northern Ireland, 1982

Plant: February to May

Harvest: second early, July to August

Type: firm

Recipe hint: boiled potatoes or potato wedges

CHARLOTTE

(bottom right) Charlotte is a very versatile variety, being most popular as a tasty salad potato. Having a long, oval shape, this waxy potato stays firm when boiled, and is also excellent sautéed or roasted in its skin.

Origin: France, 1981

Plant: February to May

Harvest: second early, July to August

Type: waxy/firm

Recipe hint: salad, boiled or roast potatoes

DESIREE

(top left) Suitable for baking, roasting or mashing, Desiree is the potato that can be all things to all people. It is the most popular red-skinned potato, with a strong flavour and a hardy constitution – it survives well in dry conditions. It has a slightly waxy texture, an oval shape, red skin and yellow flesh.

Origin: the Netherlands, 1962

Plant: March to May

Harvest: maincrop, July to October

Type: firm

Recipe hint: roast potatoes or pommes dauphinoise

DUKE OF YORK

(bottom left) Top-quality tubers transplanted from the Netherlands to Scotland at the end of the 19th century, Duke of York potatoes are pale yellow. Waxy at the start of the season, if lifted later, they have a slightly drier consistency, with a more pronounced flavour.

Origin: Scotland, 1891

Plant: January to March

Harvest: first early, from the end of May to June

Type: waxy

Recipe hint: roast potatoes

DUNDROD

A smooth, early potato, Dundrod is a good all-rounder that is best suited to boiling. If harvested a little later in the year, it makes good chips.

Origin: Northern Ireland, 1987

Plant: January to March

Harvest: first early, from the end of May to June

Type: waxy/firm

Recipe hint: boiled potatoes

ESTIMA

(right) With its mild flavour, Estima is a versatile potato that remains firm when cooked.

Origin: the Netherlands, 1973

Plant: February to May

Harvest: second early, July to August

Type: firm/waxy

Recipe hint: boiled or jacket potatoes

FIANNA

Similar to the Maris Piper (see page 91) in appearance, Fianna makes excellent chips or roast potatoes. It also stores well.

Origin: the Netherlands, 1987

Plant: March to May

Harvest: maincrop, July to October

Type: floury

Recipe hint: chips or roast potatoes

GOLDEN WONDER

A richly flavoured potato, Golden Wonder originated as an English variety called Maincrop or Langworthy. It keeps very well, and its flavour is said to improve up to two months after lifting. Golden Wonder crisps, 'the crisps bursting with flavour', were named after this particular variety.

Origin: the UK, 1906

Plant: March to May

Harvest: maincrop, July to October

Type: floury

Recipe hint: boiled or roast potatoes

HARMONY

(left) A smooth, white potato with a good, rounded shape, Harmony boils well.

Origin: Scotland, 1998

Plant: March to May

Harvest: maincrop, July to October

Type: waxy

Recipe hint: boiled potatoes

Recipe hint: boiled or roast potatoes

JERSEY ROYAL

(right) The Jersey Royal first appeared in London in 1880, and was originally called the Jersey Royal Fluke because of the circumstances in which it was grown. Hugh de la Haye, a Jersey farmer, showed his friends a potato with 15 eyes, and decided to plant it to see what would emerge. Most of the resulting crop consisted of small, round potatoes, but kidney-shaped potatoes with thin skins were also produced. De la Haye planted some more and sent his first crop to London during the 1880s, where it sold for 140 shillings a ton and was eaten with delight. By the late 1890s, the Jersey Royal crop was weighing in at 60,960,000 kg (60,000 tons). Today, the growing season is January to March, and the annual crop weighs about 40,640,000 kg (40,000 tons). During the peak harvesting season in May, up to 1,524,000 kg (1,500 tons) of Jersey Royals are exported every day from Jersey to mainland Britain.

Origin: Channel Islands, 1880

Plant: January to March

Harvest: first early, April to May

Type: firm

Recipe hint: boiled or salad potatoes

KERR'S PINK

A fine, Scottish potato, Kerr's Pink is firm to floury, and is most appreciated as part of a Burns' Night supper, being an excellent accompaniment to haggis.

Origin: Scotland, 1917

Plant: March to May

Harvest: maincrop, July to October

Type: firm/floury

Recipe hint: mashed or roast potatoes

KING EDWARD

(left) The popular King Edward potato was first grown in Northumberland, its original name ('Fellside Hero') being changed in honour of the new king's coronation in 1902. A floury spud with a white-and-pink skin, it makes excellent roast potatoes and homemade chips, as well as creamy mash.

Origin: England, 1902

Plant: March to May

Harvest: maincrop, July to October

Type: floury

Recipe hint: mashed or roast potatoes and chips

MARFONA

(right) With a really smooth texture and an almost buttery flavour, Marfona is a great baking potato. From the grower's point of view, Marfona is a high-yielding plant that produces large potatoes. Usually harvested in August, these store well and are available almost all year round.

Origin: the Netherlands, 1975

Plant: February to May

Harvest: second early, July to August

Type: waxy

Recipe hint: jacket potatoes

MARIS BARD

Maris Bard was once one of the first earlies to be harvested, and although other new potatoes are lifted even earlier, this variety is popular with gardeners. It has a good flavour and cooks well.

Origin: England, 1972

Plant: January to March

Harvest: first early, from the end of May to June

Type: waxy

Recipe hint: boiled potatoes

MARIS PEER

Small, egg-shaped potatoes, Maris Peers are ideal in salads as they have a firm texture when cooked. The plants are planted close together, and the sight of a field of Maris Peer in flower is quite beautiful: the plants have attractive, purple flowers, with a lovely scent.

Origin: England, 1962

Plant: February to May

Harvest: second early, July to August

Type: firm

Recipe hint: salad potatoes or potato wedges

MARIS PIPER

(left) One of the most ubiquitous potatoes in the UK, Maris Piper combines high yields with great flavour, and makes wonderful chips. It is probably the most widely grown variety in the UK, but is less popular with gardeners as slugs love its plants as much as we love its chips.

Origin: England, 1964

Plant: March to May

Harvest: maincrop, July to October

Type: firm

Recipe hint: chips or roast potatoes

NADINE

Versatile potatoes that are especially popular in New Zealand and Australia, Nadine potatoes are waxy, round spuds that are ideal for boiling and in salads.

Origin: Scotland, 1987

Plant: February to May

Harvest: second early, July to August

Type: waxy

Recipe hint: boiled and salad potatoes

NICOLA

(right) Nicola potatoes are similar to Charlottes (see page 76), being small, tasty, salad potatoes. They have yellow flesh and a long, oval shape.

Origin: Germany, 1973

Plant: March to May

Harvest: maincrop, July to October

Type: waxy

Recipe hint: salad potatoes

OSPREY

A high-yielding variety that has been bred to be disease-free, Osprey potatoes are waxy and ideal for boiling.

Origin: Scotland, 1999

Plant: February to May

Harvest: second early, July to August

Type: waxy

Recipe hint: boiled potatoes

PENTLAND JAVELIN

(left) Bred by one of Scotland's leading growers (Jack Dunnett), Pentland Javelin is a reliable and popular first early potato. These oval, white-skinned spuds have white flesh and an excellent flavour.

Origin: Scotland, 1968

Plant: January to March

Harvest: first early, from the end of May to June

Type: firm

Recipe hint: boiled or salad potatoes

PINK FIR APPLE

(right) With a very distinctive, long, knobbly shape and red skin, Pink Fir Apple potatoes have a superb flavour. Their skins peel off easily after boiling, and they make excellent chips – just use the whole spud!

Origin: Europe, 1850

Plant: March to May

Harvest: maincrop, July to October

Type: waxy

Recipe hint: boiled or salad potatoes and chunky chips

PREMIERE

A reliable potato, Premiere produces firm, white-fleshed tubers with an excellent flavour.

Origin: the Netherlands, 1979

Plant: January to March

Harvest: first early, from the end of May to June

Type: firm

Recipe hint: boiled potatoes

LA RATTE

Slightly less knobbly than Pink Fir Apples (see above), which they resemble in flavour, La Ratte potatoes are classics of French cooking.

Origin: Denmark or France, 1872

Plant: March to May

Harvest: maincrop, July to October

Type: waxy

Recipe hint: boiled potatoes

ROCKET

(left) Rocket potatoes grow very quickly, achieving a good-sized, round tuber. They have a mild flavour and are excellent for boiling and in salads.

Origin: England, 1987

Plant: January to March

Harvest: first early, from the end of May to June

Type: waxy/firm

Recipe hint: boiled or salad potatoes

ROMANO

(top right) Red-skinned Romano potatoes are firm, with a soft, dry texture; they make lovely potato wedges. Bred from Desiree potatoes (see page 79), they have a more uniform size, but are not so strongly flavoured.

Origin: the Netherlands, 1978

Plant: March to May

Harvest: maincrop, July to October

Type: firm

Recipe hint: potato wedges

ROOSTER

(bottom right) Rooster potatoes are regarded as good all-rounders, being suitable for chips, mash and roasting.

Origin: Ireland, 1993

Plant: March to May

Harvest: maincrop, July to October

Type: floury

Recipe hint: mashed potatoes or chips

SANTE

(left) A pebble-shaped potato, Sante has a light-yellow skin and flesh. It is disease-resistant, and is therefore popular with growers of organic produce.

Origin: the Netherlands, 1983

Plant: March to May

Harvest: maincrop, July to October

Type: floury

Recipe hint: chips or roast potatoes

SARPO MIRA

Originating in Hungary, Sarpo varieties produce huge yields, resist disease and taste terrific.

Origin: Hungary, 2003

Plant: March to May

Harvest: maincrop, July to October

Type: floury

Recipe hint: boiled, baked, mashed or salad potatoes

WILJA

With a firm, slightly dry texture, Wilja potatoes are good for roasting, mashing and boiling. They also make delicious chips.

Origin: the Netherlands, 1967

Plant: February to May

Harvest: second early, July to August

Type: firm

Recipe hint: mashed potatoes

Micro-plants and mini-tubers

Many 'heritage' varieties of potatoes are preserved as micro-plants, which are grown from tuber cells in laboratory conditions to ensure disease-free plants, while mini-tubers are grown from micro-plants. Once established, the micro-plants are grown on in compost. They can be planted out as normal, but may be susceptible to potato cyst nematode (PCN), so it is best to grown them in a growbag. They produce normal-sized tubers. Varieties include Shetland Black (right), Fortyfold and Highland Burgundy Red.

Late maincrop Fortyfold, a purple-skinned, deep-eyed tuber, is one of the oldest varieties available and dates back to 1836. The Victorians prized these potatoes because of their tremendously high yields, and, even by today's standards, Fortyfold produces large numbers of tubers. It is a difficult variety to grow commercially because the tubers vary tremendously in size, but it is a wonderful potato for the gardener, with a slightly nutty taste.

Shetland Black (right) is a striking potato, with dark-purple – almost black – skin, which legend says was introduced to the UK via a wrecked ship of the Spanish Armada in 1588. With their floury, pale-yellow flesh and distinctive, purple vascular ring, these second early potatoes are versatile bakers and roasters.

CULTIVATING POTATOES

With a little planning, preparation and care, it should not be difficult to grow your own spuds.

Planting potatoes

In ideal conditions, potatoes are grown in a well-dug trench in the garden, but for those without the space, a 40-litre container (such as an old bin) will produce equally good results. There are many potato-growing kits available in garden centres and from specialist gardening websites that also supply a variety of containers and a wide selection of potatoes. If space is tight, try growing early potatoes as they are smaller and less prone to pest problems (simply because they are lifted earlier in the year, before such pests as slugs are active).

If you can plan well ahead, it is also worth working out when you should harvest the spuds to make sure that this will not coincide with your annual holiday away from home!

SEED POTATOES

Many of us inadvertently produce our own seed potatoes simply by neglecting old spuds in the vegetable rack in the kitchen, but this is not recommended as the best way to acquire a quality crop. Almost any potato will begin to sprout in the right conditions, but it is better if you begin with potatoes that are certified disease-free. So buy seed potatoes from a reputable garden centre or specialist supplier and look out for ones that are certified disease-free, with high yields. It is also possible to purchase pre-chitted tubers that can be planted out directly.

You will probably notice that one end of each seed potato is rounder and more blunt than the other – note that this end should remain pointing upwards when planting in order to encourage it to sprout.

From late January (about six weeks before planting them), put your seed potatoes in a planting tray or old box, blunt ends pointing upwards, to encourage them to 'chit', or sprout. Leave them in a cool spot, with plenty of natural light, to encourage the growth of strong chits. Some of the potatoes may turn a little green, but this is not a cause for concern. The warmer the room, the quicker the chitting will occur. The potatoes are ready for planting out once the shoots are 1.5–2.5 cm long. This process will probably take about two weeks.

Encourage the growth of larger, but fewer, tubers by removing any side shoots, leaving just the main chit. If you want more numerous, but smaller, spuds, however, leave all of the shoots and plant the potato on its side.

PLANTING OUT POTATOES

Potatoes can be planted out as soon as the ground can be worked in the spring, but they will not begin to grow until the earth has reached a temperature of 5.5°C. The soil should be moist, but not too wet or soggy; if the earth is too wet, the potatoes will simply rot. Potato plants are pretty hardy, but if there is any danger of more than a light frost, it is advisable to protect the plants with a plastic covering or a layer of straw. In the UK, the ideal planting time is between March and May, when there is little danger of a late frost damaging the plants.

Try to plant your potatoes on a site that receives full sun. It should be well drained, with a soil pH of between 5.0 and 6.0 – alkaline or limey soils encourage potato scab. It is important not to use the same piece of ground more than once every three years. Rotate the crops in your garden to minimise the problem of pests – if the pests that thrive on potatoes have none to feed on, they will die off.

Potatoes can be planted out whole, but you can also chop larger seed potatoes into 'seeds'; each seed should be around 2.5 cm square, with one or two 'eyes' or 'buds'. Frankly, it is a lot easier just to plant the potatoes in one piece.

Potatoes are prolific plants and therefore require a healthy level of nutrients in the soil within which they are growing. When you are preparing your potato patch, figure on adding about 20 kg of manure per square metre of land to ensure that there is plenty of nitrogen in the soil. Potash is another necessary nutrient, so if you have a wood fire, or have recently had a bonfire of garden rubbish, dig in some of the ash as it is a valuable resource.

Prepare the ground by digging over the designated potato patch, incorporating plenty of well-rotted compost – but not too much, or you'll risk encouraging potato scab. Make sure that any weeds or stones have been removed. The potatoes can then be planted, eye side pointing upwards, before being covered with a thick layer of soil. They should be spaced at least 30 cm apart.

This is a perfectly sufficient method, but a more organised (and traditional) one is to dig a trench to spade depth and add a light sprinkling of fertiliser along the bottom – about 60 g per metre of trench. Then plant the potatoes or seeds every 30 cm or so for early varieties, and every 45 cm for maincrop ones. If you have more than one trench, they should be about 45–60 cm apart. If the plants are too close, the tubers' growth will be restricted. And if they are too far apart, valuable growing space is wasted, giving weeds more of a chance to flourish. When planting, consider the final size of the variety and adjust distances accordingly. Handle the tubers carefully and plant them with the shoots pointing upwards. Then cover the seeds with the earth dug from the trench.

CONTAINER PLANTING

About five seed potatoes will produce a reasonable crop when grown in a 40-litre container. Use a container that is at least 30 cm deep, with adequate drainage holes in the bottom. Half-fill it with multi-purpose compost or good-quality garden soil. Pop two seed potatoes on top of the compost, eyes facing upwards, then top up the container with more soil or compost, to within an inch of the rim.

The compost in the container must be kept moist and fertilised. The young plants do not require too much water at first, but once they are 45 cm high, they will need daily watering, or else both the yield and the quality of the crop will suffer. Potato plants like plenty of sun, so bear that in mind when choosing where to position the container. Once the shoots emerge, look after them in the same way that you would potatoes planted in the ground.

EARTHING UP

After about two weeks, depending on the soil temperature, sprouts should begin to emerge from your potatoes. Once the plants are about 15 cm high, earth up the potato drills by using a hoe to pile up soil around the base of each plant. The aim is to form a peaked ridge over the emerging shoot with loose soil around the edge of the trench. This ensures that the tubers remain covered, without being exposed to the light (and thus do not turn green and inedible), and helps to improve drainage and ventilation around the plants. You may need to add 2.5 to 5 cm of soil every week to keep the growing potatoes covered.

Two or three weeks after the first earthing-up, repeat the process, adding soil halfway up the stem of each plant. Try not to cover too much of the leafy matter as this may reduce the final yield of the crop.

WATERING, FLOWERING AND CARE

Unless there is regular rainfall, the potato plants will need daily watering, especially once they are in flower. Not all varieties of potatoes produce flowering plants, but if and when the first flowers appear, it is a sign that there are edible tubers beneath the soil. When the foliage turns yellow and dies back, you can ease off your watering regime to allow the potatoes to mature before harvesting.

The plants will benefit from the application of proprietary fertilisers throughout the growing season, particularly when the plant canopy is at its widest.

HARVESTING AND STORING

When a potato plant's foliage begins to die back – which should occur eight to twelve weeks after planting – this is a clear sign that the tubers are ready to be lifted. You can begin to harvest potatoes two to three weeks after the plants have finished flowering, but you will probably find only

small tubers under each plant. It is possible to loosen the earth around the plant and pull out the larger tubers, leaving the others to mature. If the variety is not a flowering type, feel underneath the plant eight to ten weeks after planting to establish how the tubers are growing. If you wait for another couple of weeks for the foliage to die back, you will find much larger potatoes that are more suitable for storage. But if the foliage shows no sign of dying back by the end of September, cut it off and leave the crop to mature for two weeks before lifting your potatoes.

To harvest your spuds, carefully dig about 30 cm away from the plant and lift out the potatoes. Try to avoid bashing or bruising them with your spade or fork. Make sure that you clear out all of the potatoes – even the tiny ones – because any potatoes left in the ground will act as a conduit for pests and diseases.

First earlies are best eaten immediately as they do not store well. Second earlies can also be eaten fresh, but they will store well and will retain their flavour for several weeks if kept in the right conditions. When harvesting maincrop potatoes, check that the skins have set properly – the skin should be firm and dry in order to protect the potato and stop it from drying out.

If the weather is fine, leave the potatoes outside to dry for two or three days, to allow the skins to mature. If it is wet, however, move them to a dry area, such as a shed or garage. Once the skins have toughened, the potatoes can then be stored in a sack or box somewhere cool and dark. Remember that potatoes will turn green and bitter once they are exposed to light, and that if they are properly dried and stored, they should last from three to six months.

The best way to store potatoes is in a hessian sack (these can be purchased from specialist potato-seed suppliers). Do not try to store them in plastic sacks as they will simply rot – if they are to be preserved, potatoes need air circulating around them. It is worth sorting through the potatoes to remove any that have been damaged by spades or slugs. And if you suspect that blight has infected any, remove them because blight can spread through a crop of stored potatoes.

The potatoes should be stored at a temperature of about 5°C in a cool, dark garage or shed. (Bring them into the house for a few days before using them.) It is worth emptying out the sack every few weeks to check on the potatoes. If they have begun to rot, you will probably be able to smell it before you actually find the damaged tubers.

Diseases and pests

Potato plants are susceptible to a number of diseases, and may be attacked by pests. Some of the most common are listed below. Note that a few potato diseases are irritatingly ineradicable, and that the best way to combat them is to select potatoes that have been bred to be disease-resistant.

SLUGS

(left). Guard against slugs by adding slug pellets to the potato trench when you first dig it – because slugs live underground, this may limit their activity. It is also important to harvest potatoes as quickly as possible because slug numbers increase dramatically in late summer, just when your prized potatoes are ready to be lifted.

BLIGHT

Blight is a fungal condition that thrives in high humidity and mild temperatures throughout the mid-summer and autumn. Early signs are the emergence of small, dark patches on the potato plant's leaves, with a yellowish border spreading across the leaves, or dark patches on the stem where the leaves join it. If your plant is infected, the tubers will be discoloured and will rot, so it is best to chop down the foliage and dispose of it in a covered compost bin, or else to burn the plants. Rain and wind will help to spread the spores by washing them down the plant and into the soil, as well as across fields. To prevent blight, spray your plants with a fungicide.(right)

BLACKLEG

Blackleg is a soft-rot bacterial disease that infects the bottom of the potato stem near the soil, turning it black and causing it to decompose. This rot quickly spreads to the potatoes. The leaves also turn yellow and the whole plant then slumps and dies as it can no longer absorb any nutrients from the soil. Blackleg is more common in cold, wet conditions. The tubers may appear healthy when they are lifted, but will rot if stored, and note that the infection can be spread in storage. (Picture p130).

COMMON SCAB

Common scab is caused by a fungus, often after a period of hot, dry weather is followed by heavy watering. Potatoes planted in limed soil, or in alkaline earth with a high pH value, are more susceptible. Scab can be unsightly, causing warty, scab-like growths on tubers, but it does not affect the yield of the plant, and the tubers are perfectly edible, even though they may have patches of cork-like tissue on the surface.

POWDERY SCAB

Powdery scab is a fungal infection that flourishes in cool, wet conditions. Its spores can live in the soil for several years, and the infection is visible on a potato plant's roots as small, tumorous growths. The tubers themselves carry the infection.

POTATO CYST NEMATODE (PCN)

Potato cyst nematode (PCN) is caused by microscopic eelworms that are all but invisible to the naked eye. They live off potato plants, burrowing into them through the root system, and stunt the plant's growth. The foliage wilts and turns yellow, and the tuber yields are poor. Their eggs can survive in the soil for years, so the only way to reduce the risk of infestation is to grow PCN-resistant varieties.

COOKING AND NUTRITION

Delicious when cooked properly, raw potatoes can actually kill you. Potatoes have natural defences against fungi and insects to protect the growing plants, and the leaves, stem and sprouting parts contain high levels of toxic glycoalkaloids. Although the tuber only has low levels of it, green potato skins contain the toxin solanine, which is poisonous. If potatoes are exposed to light, they turn green, partly because levels of chlorophyll increase, but also as an indication of high levels of solanine and chaconine. So it's important to cut out any green parts of your potatoes before cooking them as cooking will not destroy the toxins.

Potatoes contain a variety of vitamins and minerals that provide an excellent base for a healthy diet. They are a useful source of starch and carbohydrates, and are rich in calcium and protein. One medium-sized potato contains half the adult daily requirement of vitamin C. They are 80 per cent

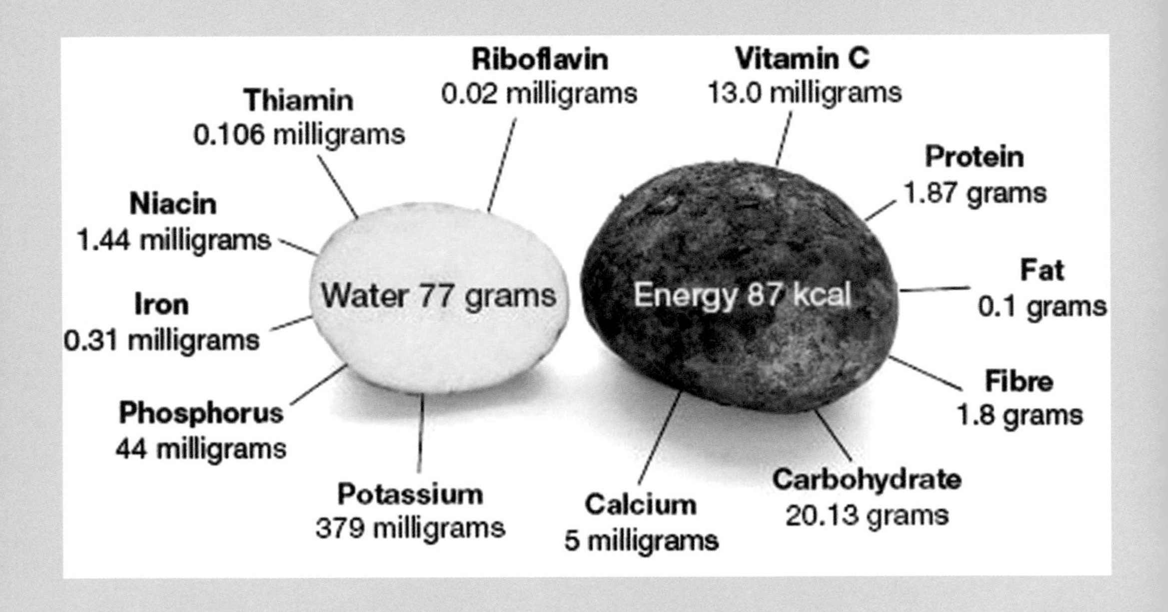
Riboflavin
0.02 milligrams
Vitamin C
13.0 milligrams
Thiamin
0.106 milligrams
Protein
1.87 grams
Niacin
1.44 milligrams
Fat
0.1 grams
Water 77 grams
Energy 87 kcal
Iron
0.31 milligrams
Fibre
1.8 grams
Phosphorus
44 milligrams
Potassium
379 milligrams
Calcium
5 milligrams
Carbohydrate
20.13 grams

water and 20 per cent solid, each medium-sized spud providing about 110 calories, which includes 3 g of protein, virtually no fat and no cholesterol. A 225 g serving of boiled potatoes provides about 160 calories, but if you add just 1 tablespoon of butter, the number of calories doubles. Potatoes are an important source of B vitamins, providing 30 per cent of the recommended daily allowance of B6. Rich in potassium and iron, a baked potato contains the same amount of fibre as two slices of wholemeal bread. Potatoes supply more iron than any other vegetable, and, if eaten with the skin, supply about 10 per cent of a person's recommended daily intake of fibre.

Most of the vitamins and minerals are just under a potato's skin, so leave the skin on to absorb their benefit. Even if you don't like the skin, try cooking potatoes in their skins and then removing the skin just before you eat it – that way, the nutrients remain in the potato while it is being cooked.

Preserving potatoes

If properly stored, potatoes can last for several months and still remain edible – indeed, this is one of their strengths as a peasant food. Essentially, they need to be kept somewhere cool and dark – if they are exposed to too much daylight, they will turn green and become bitter. When buying potatoes to store, look for a firm, smooth skin that is not crinkled, and avoid potatoes that are turning green or growing sprouts. If you buy potatoes in a plastic bag, it is best to remove them from this before storing them. Plastic will encourage the formation of moisture and heat, so try to store your potatoes in paper or in a cloth bag.

Mrs Beeton recommends four different methods of preservation, stressing the need for strict control of temperature: too hot, and the potatoes will sprout or rot; too cold, and they will rot in the frost. Interestingly, the favoured method seems to be to return them to the ground: 'Another mode is to scoop out the eyes with a very small scoop, and keep the roots buried in earth . . . bury them so deep in dry soil, that no change of temperature will reach them; and thus, being without air, they will remain upwards of a year without vegetating'.

Cooking potatoes

When choosing how to cook your spuds, first make sure that you have the right potato for the job. There are over four hundred varieties to choose from, although only about thirty are grown commercially in large quantities. Different varieties have different characteristics, but in general, potatoes are either waxy or floury: waxy potatoes remain firm when cooked and are good for boiling and for use in salads; floury potatoes fluff up beautifully for chips, mashed, roast or baked potatoes. Experts can tell the difference between the flavours of the different varieties.

Mrs Beeton notes several ways of cooking 'this wholesome and delicious vegetable', giving precise instructions to the novice cook. In her book, she also includes a few more slightly unusual uses: potatoes can be used to clean linen just as well as soap, she says, and she alleges that the berries from the potato plant were once used for exactly this purpose in Peru.

BOILED POTATOES

To boil potatoes, first chose potatoes of a similar size, or cut them into equal-sized pieces. The potatoes can be peeled or simply scrubbed before boiling, but they will retain more goodness if they are cooked with their skins on. And new potatoes are tastier if left unpeeled. To peel a boiled potato, allow it to cool slightly after cooking, then hold it in a clean tea towel and squeeze it gently to remove the skin.

Baby new potatoes take about 12 minutes to boil, and small potatoes, about 15 to 20 minutes, while large, quartered potatoes take about 20 minutes. Make sure that the pan is covered while you are boiling the potatoes in order to retain the heat and reduce the cooking time. After about 15 minutes, pierce one of the potatoes with a skewer or knife. If the skewer slips in easily, the potatoes are done.

MASHED POTATOES

You can't beat a bowl of fluffy mash! Having made sure that you are using floury potatoes, first peel them and then cut them into equal-sized chunks. Now boil them for 20 minutes, or until they are done. Then drain the potatoes and return them to the pan, leaving it over a gentle heat for a minute or so to allow any excess moisture to evaporate. Add a knob of butter, a dash of milk, some salt and pepper and either mash the potatoes with a potato masher or force them through a potato ricer. (Note that if you cook the potatoes in their skins, the resulting mash will be a little drier and so better able to take up additional liquids and flavourings.)

BAKED POTATOES

Baked potatoes smell wonderful while they are cooking, and the contrast between their crispy skins and fluffy insides is a gastronomic treat. They can be served as a side dish or as a simple meal in themselves, perhaps with a favourite topping, such as tuna, cheese or baked beans.

To prepare baked potatoes, first choose equal-sized potatoes and then scrub and dry them. Prick the skins all over, which will allow steam to escape from the potato during cooking and should prevent the spud from bursting. If the potatoes are quite large, slide them on to a metal skewer, which will help to disperse the heat through the middle of the potato. Then bake the potatoes in the oven at a temperature of 200°C/400°F/Gas 6 for 1 to 1 ½ hours until tender.

Baked potatoes can be cooked more quickly in a microwave oven, but unless you finish them off for 15 minutes or so in a conventional oven, you will not achieve delicious, crispy skins. If using a microwave, first prepare the potatoes by scrubbing and pricking them, and then cook them on high. One potato will take 8 to 10 minutes; two, about 15 minutes; and four, 20 to 25 minutes. Turn the potatoes halfway through the cooking time to ensure that they are cooked evenly.

ROAST POTATOES

Floury potatoes make the best roast potatoes, with a crisp outer surface and a fluffy inside. Peel the potatoes and cut them into equal-sized pieces to ensure that they cook evenly. Now par-boil the potatoes for 10 minutes. Meanwhile, make sure that a roasting tin is warming in the oven at a temperature of 200°C/400°F/Gas 6. Coat the roasting tin with vegetable oil (sunflower, groundnut or blended) or, for extra flavour, use goose fat, dripping or lard, and preheat the tin for at least five minutes. (If there is space around your joint of pork, beef or lamb, you could roast a few potatoes alongside the meat for an even better flavour, although note that they are likely to absorb some of the meat juices and will then become soggy.)

At the end of the par-boiling time, drain the potatoes and return them to the saucepan. Give them a good shake to roughen their surfaces, then remove the roasting tin from the oven and tip the potatoes into the fat. Return them to the oven for about an hour, turning them once during the cooking time.

Waxy new potatoes are also delicious when roasted in their skins in olive oil, with a scattering of rosemary over the top. Being generally smaller than floury potatoes, they will take about 45 minutes to roast.

POTATO WEDGES

If you've run out of oven chips, potato wedges make a delicious, healthy alternative. Oil a roasting tin and preheat it in the oven for five minutes. In the meantime, scrub, but do not bother to peel, three or four large, floury potatoes. Then slice them into wedges – cut each large potato into eighths – and roast them in the oven for 25 to 30 minutes, at a temperature of 200°C/400°F/Gas

HOMEMADE CHIPS

Yes, they are fiddly to make, and the smell of oil can permeate the house, but nothing can beat really good homemade chips. The secret lies in heating the oil to the right temperature and then maintaining it for long enough to cook a batch of chips. If it is too cool, the chips will absorb the oil and will become soggy; if it is too hot, the chips will burn on the outside and will remain hard on the inside. To make chips at home, you could either use a conventional chip pan on top of the stove or invest in a deep fat fryer, which lessens the cooking smell.

First, peel and slice the potatoes into equal-sized chips. Then pat them dry with kitchen paper to remove as much moisture as possible. Heat the oil in the chip pan or deep fat fryer to a temperature of 180–190°C (350–375°F). Add some chips to the basket before lowering it into the oil. Do not overcrowd the chips – leave them room in which to sizzle and colour evenly – and note that you will probably need to cook them in several batches. When they are done, tip them on to some absorbent kitchen paper to remove the excess oil. Keep them warm while you cook the remainder of the chips.

SHALLOW-FRIED POTATOES

Shallow-frying potatoes is a great way to use up leftover boiled or roasted potatoes. Simply slice the cooked potatoes into small chunks and then sauté the spuds in a heavy-bottomed frying pan. They are delicious as part of a Spanish omelette or as a side dish.

Vichyssoise

This classic dish is traditionally served cold and has a delicate flavour. It should be passed through a sieve after puréeing to ensure a really smooth texture. If you do not like chilled soups (my children will not even try them), you can serve it warm, when it becomes the less glamorous sounding, but nonetheless delicious, leek and potato soup. In this case, you can omit passing the soup through a sieve as a rougher texture is fine for a hot soup.

Ingredients for 2

2 large leeks
25g/1oz butter
1 shallot, chopped
225g/8oz floury potatoes, peeled and diced
375ml/13fl oz good chicken or vegetable stock
1 bay leaf
2 sprigs parsley
75ml/2½fl oz double cream
salt and white pepper
fresh chives to garnish

Ingredients for 4

4 large leeks
50g/2oz butter
2 shallots, chopped
450g/1lb floury potatoes, peeled and diced
750ml/1¼pt good chicken or vegetable stock
1 bay leaf
2 sprigs parsley
150ml/¼pt double cream
salt and white pepper
fresh chives, to garnish

1 Trim the leeks and discard the green parts. Slit the leeks lengthwise and wash out the dirt. Shake them dry and then chop finely.

2 Melt the butter in a saucepan and gently sauté the shallots for a few minutes until softened.

3 Stir in the leeks and potatoes and cook gently, stirring frequently, for 10 minutes.

4 Add the stock and herbs and bring to the boil. Reduce the heat, cover and simmer for 30 minutes. Stir in the cream.

5 Allow to cool slightly and then purée in a liquidizer. Strain through a sieve. Allow to cool completely and then chill until required.

6 Check the seasoning and add a little salt and white pepper if required. Serve garnished with fresh chives.

Potato Soup with Roasted Garlic and Parsley

This has to be one of the tastiest soups I make and yet it is made from the most humble of ingredients. This recipe gives a mildly garlic flavour but if you are a garlic fan feel free to increase the amount of garlic. There is no need to peel the garlic before roasting, just squeeze it out of the skin as you add it to the pan.

Ingredients for 2

3 to 4 cloves garlic
1 tbsp extra virgin olive oil
1 small onion, chopped
350g/12oz potatoes, peeled and diced
450ml/3/4pt vegetable or chicken stock
salt and freshly ground black pepper
a little grated nutmeg
4 tbsp chopped fresh parsley
50g/2oz diced pancetta (optional)

Ingredients for 4

4 to 8 cloves garlic
2 tbsp extra virgin olive oil
1 large onion, chopped
700g/1 1/2lb potatoes, peeled and diced
900ml/1 1/2pt vegetable or chicken stock
salt and freshly ground black pepper
a little grated nutmeg
4 tbsp chopped fresh parsley
75g/3oz diced pancetta (optional)

2

3

1 Preheat the oven to 200°C/400°F/gas mark 6. Place the garlic cloves on a baking tray and roast for 10–20 minutes until soft.

2 Heat the olive oil in a saucepan and fry the onion and potatoes for 10 minutes until soft.

3 Allow the garlic to cool slightly and then squeeze it from the skins into the pan.

4 Add the stock and bring to the boil. Reduce the heat and simmer for 20 minutes.

5 Purée the soup in a liquidizer or food processor and return to the pan. Season with salt, pepper and nutmeg.

6 Stir in the parsley and serve.

7 If desired, serve with a garnish of pancetta cubes, fried until crisp.

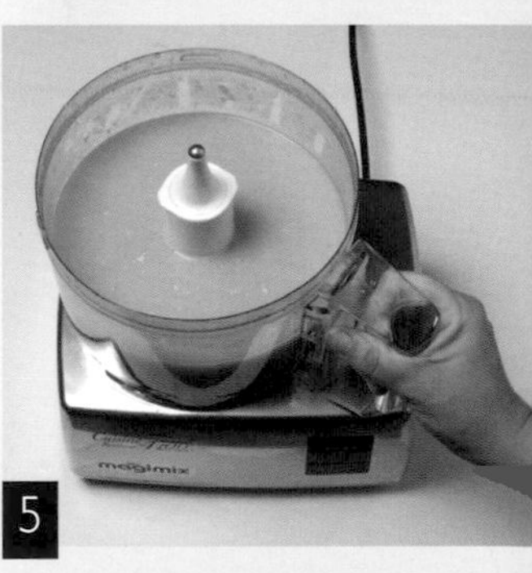

5

Curried Potato Soup

You can have this soup cooked and ready to eat in about 30 minutes, making it a great midweek meal. I like to serve it with naan bread and coriander chutney.

Ingredients for 2

- 1 tbsp sunflower oil
- 1 small onion, chopped
- 1 clove garlic, chopped
- 150g/5oz floury potatoes, peeled and diced
- 1–2 tsp medium or mild curry paste
- 450ml/¾pt vegetable stock
- 50g/2oz frozen peas
- 25g/1oz small spinach leaves
- 3 tbsp natural yoghurt

Ingredients for 4

- 2 tbsp sunflower oil
- 1 large onion, chopped
- 2 cloves garlic, chopped
- 275g/10oz floury potatoes, peeled and diced
- 1 tbsp medium or mild curry paste
- 900ml/1½pt vegetable stock
- 100g/4oz frozen peas
- 50g/2oz small spinach leaves
- 6 tbsp natural yoghurt

1 Heat the oil in a large saucepan and fry the onion for 3–4 minutes until beginning to soften.

2 Add the garlic and potatoes and fry gently, stirring constantly, for 5 minutes.

3 Stir in the curry paste and cook for 1 minute, stirring.

4 Stir in the stock and bring to the boil. Reduce the heat, cover and simmer for about 15 minutes until the potato begins to break up.

5 Add the peas and spinach and cook for a further 5 minutes.

6 Remove from the heat and stir in the natural yoghurt. Serve immediately.

Rösti Tartlets with Tomatoes and Goat's Cheese

The crisp, potato-based tartlet cases make an unusual alternative to this fashionable starter.

Ingredients for 2	Ingredients for 4
225g/8oz waxy potatoes, peeled	450g/1lb waxy potatoes, peeled
1 tbsp flour	2 tbsp flour
2 tbsp beaten egg	1 egg, lightly beaten
100g/4oz vine-ripened tomatoes, sliced	200g/7oz vine-ripened tomatoes, sliced
a few black olives	a few black olives
2 slices peppered goat's cheese	4 slices peppered goat's cheese
2 tsp extra virgin olive oil	1 tbsp extra virgin olive oil
1 tsp balsamic vinegar	2 tsp balsamic vinegar
salt and freshly ground black pepper	salt and freshly ground black pepper

1 Preheat the oven to 200°C/400°F/gas mark 6.

2 Coarsely grate the potatoes and place in a sieve. Put a small plate on the potatoes and press down, squeezing out as much moisture as you can.

3 Place the potatoes in a bowl and season with salt and pepper.

4 Sprinkle over the flour and add the egg. Mix well.

5 Divide the potatoes equally between two (four) shallow Yorkshire pudding tins, press the potato out with the back of a spoon to form a small tartlet case.

6 Bake for 20 minutes.

7 Arrange the tomato slices and olives in each tartlet case and return to the oven for 10 minutes, until the potatoes are crisp and the tomatoes softened.

8 Top with the goat's cheese. Drizzle with the olive oil and balsamic vinegar and serve.

2

4

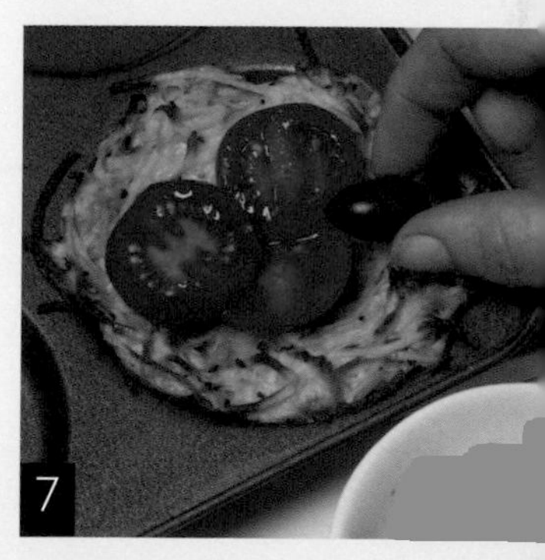

7

Potato Blinis with Smoked Trout

The blinis can be kept warm on a plate over a pan of gently simmering water. They are ideal as a starter or as part of a hot buffet. If you use mashed potato that has had butter or milk added, you will need to add less liquid to the mixture. Smoked mackerel or smoked trout are also delicious with these little pancakes.

Ingredients for 2

150g/5oz mashed potatoes
1 egg
25g/1oz plain flour
about 2 tbsp milk
15g/½oz butter, melted
salt and freshly ground black pepper
a little olive oil
50g/2oz hot smoked trout
crème fraîche, to serve
chives, to garnish

Ingredients for 4

250g/9oz mashed potatoes
2 eggs
50g/2oz plain flour
about 4 tbsp milk
25g/1oz butter, melted
salt and freshly ground black pepper
a little olive oil
100g/4oz hot smoked trout
crème fraîche, to serve
chives, to garnish

1 Place the potato in a mixing bowl. Beat the egg, flour, milk and melted butter into the potato until well combined. Season with salt and pepper.

2 Heat a little oil in a heavy-based frying pan to grease the pan. Spoon heaped tablespoons of the mixture into the pan and spread to form a small circle.

3 Cook for about 2 minutes until the underside is golden. Flip over and cook the other side.

4 Repeat with the remaining mixture until all the pancakes are made.

5 Serve the pancakes topped with a little smoked trout and a dollop of crème fraîche. Garnish with chives.

Mini Baked Potatoes with Rouille

Baked potatoes may be an all-time favourite, but here they are given a modern twist. You will find baby baking potatoes in the supermarket. Alternatively, choose small floury potatoes. The rouille will keep for up to 3 days in the refrigerator.

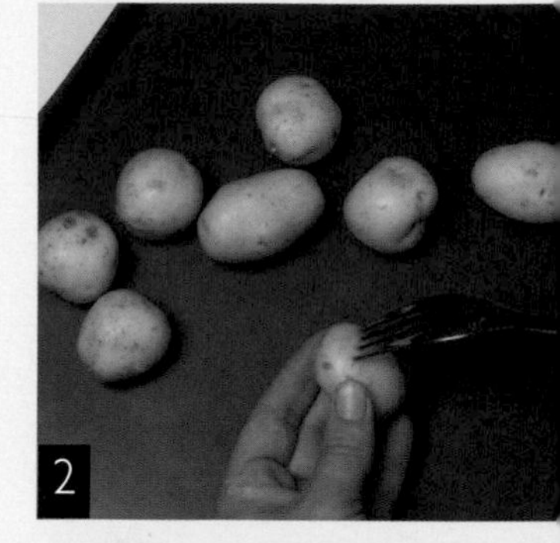

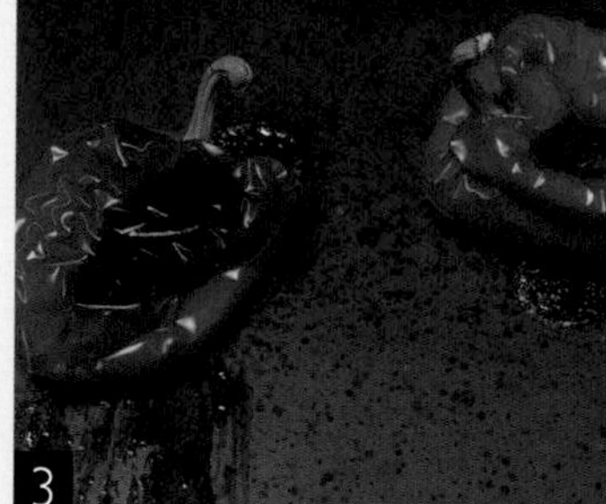

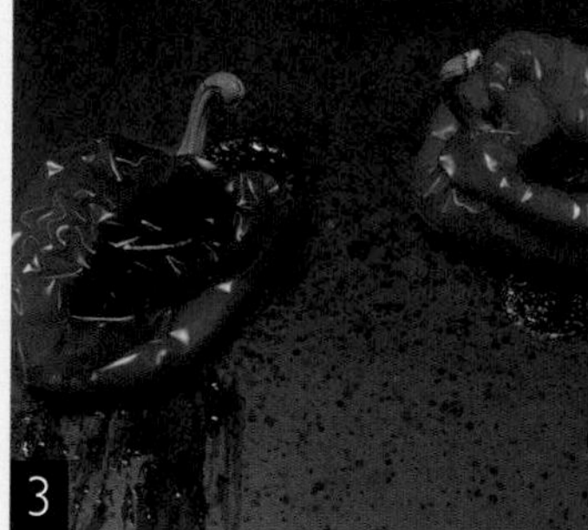

Ingredients for 2

12 baby baking potatoes
1 red pepper
1 red chilli, seeded if desired
1 clove garlic
1 tbsp fresh white breadcrumbs
1 tbsp extra virgin olive oil

Ingredients for 4

24 baby baking potatoes
2 red peppers
1 red chilli, seeded if desired
2 cloves garlic
2 tbsp fresh white breadcrumbs
2 tbsp extra virgin olive oil

1 Preheat the oven to 190°C/375°F/gas mark 5.

2 Scrub the potatoes, if required. Prick once or twice with a fork and place on a baking sheet. Bake for 40–45 minutes.

3 Meanwhile, place the peppers on a baking sheet and bake for 25 minutes at the top of the oven until the skins begin to blacken.

4 Place in a bowl, cover and leave for 5 minutes. Peel the skin and discard, together with the core and seeds, but try to keep as much of the juice as possible.

5 Place the peppers, any juice, red chilli and garlic in a food processor and process until smooth. Add the breadcrumbs and oil and process again.

6 Serve the potatoes on cocktail sticks for dipping into the rouille. Alternatively, cut a small slice off each potato and spoon the rouille on top.

Potato Skins with Roasted Tomato Salsa

Both the salsa and the potato skins can be made in advance up to the end of step 5. They will then keep for up to 24 hours in the refrigerator. Use the potato flesh for any recipe requiring mash. Smoked paprika has a distinctive aroma and flavour, which works well in this salsa, but regular paprika can also be used.

Ingredients for 2

3 medium potatoes, scrubbed
75g/3oz plum tomatoes
25g/1oz spring onions, sliced
extra virgin olive oil
1 tsp lime juice
1/4 tsp smoked paprika

Ingredients for 4

5 large potatoes, scrubbed
150g/5oz plum tomatoes
50g/2oz spring onions, sliced
extra virgin olive oil
2 tsp lime juice
1/2 tsp smoked paprika

2

1 Preheat the oven to 190°C/375°F/gas mark 5. Prick the potato all over with a fork and bake for 1–1 1/4 hours until tender.

2 Meanwhile, cut the tomatoes in half and scoop out the seeds and discard. Dice the flesh. Place on a small baking sheet with the spring onions.

3 Drizzle with a little of the olive oil and roast below the potatoes for 15 minutes.

4 Transfer to a bowl and stir in the lime juice and paprika. Chill until required.

5 When the potatoes are cooked, leave to cool for a few minutes and then cut each into quarters lengthways. Scoop out the flesh with a spoon leaving just a small layer on the skin.

6 Brush the insides and outsides of the potato skins with olive oil and return to the oven for 20 minutes, or until crisp. Serve with the tomato salsa.

4

6

Skinny Fries with Basil and Sun-blushed Tomato Dip

This is an indulgent snack that I like to serve as an occasional treat while watching a great film on the telly. Any leftover dip can be stored in the refrigerator for up to 2 days. The dip is fabulous in a ham and salad sarnie.

1

Fries for 2

2 large floury potatoes, peeled
sunflower or ground nut oil for deep-frying
sea salt

Fries for 4

4 large floury potatoes, peeled
sunflower or ground nut oil for deep-frying
sea salt

Basil & Sun-blushed Tomato Dip:

25g/1oz fresh basil leaves
25g/1oz sun-blushed tomatoes, chopped
6 tbsp mayonnaise
4 tbsp natural yoghurt

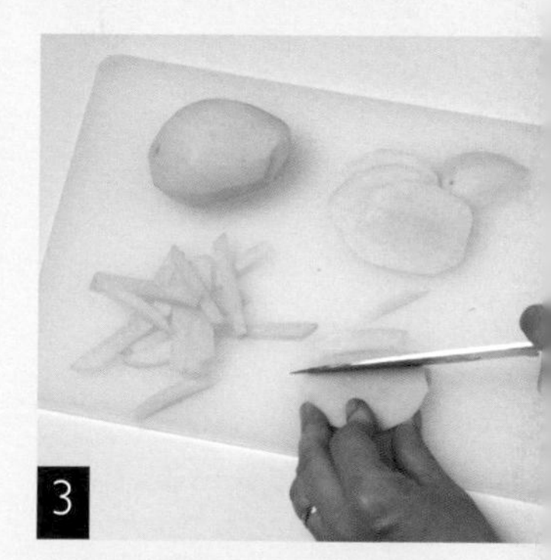

3

1 Make the dip by placing all the ingredients in a food processor and whizzing until blended.

2 Transfer to a serving bowl and chill until required.

3 Cut the potatoes into 6mm/¼in thick strips. Rinse in a colander to remove excess starch and pat dry on a clean tea towel.

4 Heat the oil to 190°C/375°F and cook the chips in two or three batches for about 5 minutes until golden brown.

5 Drain on kitchen paper and sprinkle with a little salt. Serve with the basil and sun-blushed tomato dip.

4

Mixed Potato Crisps

The hand-fried crisps available in the shops taste great but are expensive. Why not make your own? If you have a deep-fat fryer its very easy. I like to use a mixture of regular and sweet potatoes; occasionally I also fry slices of parsnip, beetroot and carrot.

Ingredients for 2

200g/7oz potatoes
100g/4oz sweet potatoes
oil for deep-frying
1/4 tsp dried thyme
sea salt, preferably Maldon
freshly ground black pepper

Ingredients for 4

400g/14oz potatoes
200g/7oz sweet potatoes
oil for deep-frying
1/2 tsp dried thyme
sea salt, preferably Maldon
freshly ground black pepper

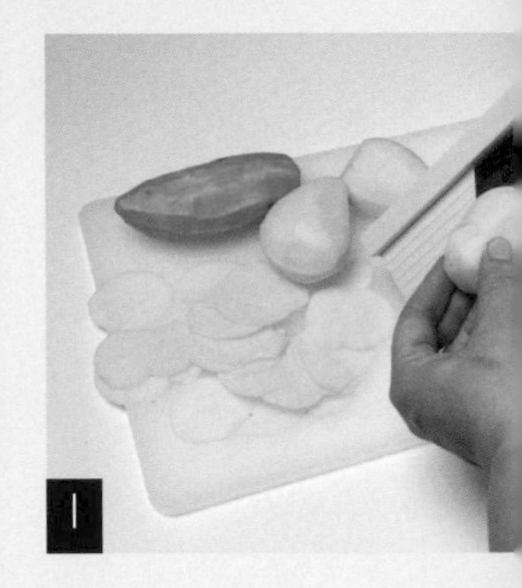

1

1 Peel the potatoes and cut into very thin slices with a sharp knife, a mandolin or in a food processor.

2 Heat the oil for deep-fat frying to 190°C/375°F.

3 Deep-fry the potato slices in batches for 2–3 minutes until crisp and golden.

4 Remove the basket from the oil and shake off any excess oil. Tip the crisps onto a tray lined with kitchen paper.

5 Serve sprinkled with dried thyme, salt and pepper.

3

4

Smoked Mackerel and Dill Salad

Serve as a light main meal salad or serve smaller portions as a starter to a meal.

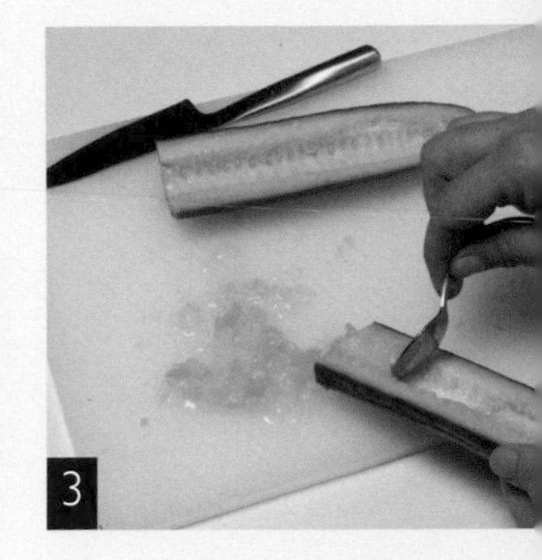
3

Ingredients for 2	Ingredients for 4
450g/1lb new potatoes	900g/2lb new potatoes
100g/4oz cucumber	200g/7oz cucumber
200g/7oz smoked peppered mackerel	400g/14oz smoked peppered mackerel
2 tbsp olive oil	4 tbsp olive oil
2 tbsp white wine vinegar	4 tbsp white wine vinegar
1 tbsp chopped fresh dill	2 tbsp chopped fresh dill
sea salt	sea salt

1 Place the potatoes in a saucepan and add enough water to just cover. Cover the pan, place over a high heat and bring to the boil.

2 Salt the water, reduce the heat and simmer for 15–20 minutes until just tender. Drain well. Halve or quarter, depending on the size.

3 Cut the cucumber in half lengthwise and scoop out the seeds. Peel, if desired. Cut in half again lengthwise, then cut into 1cm/½in thick slices. Add to the potatoes.

4 Flake the fish into large chunks. Add to the potatoes.

5 Whisk together the oil, vinegar and dill. Pour over the potatoes and toss to coat. Take care not to break up the fish too much. Serve immediately.

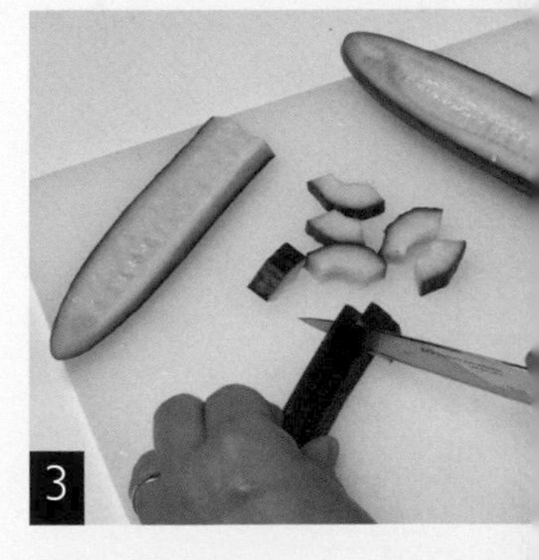
3

4

New Potato Salad with Red Onion Dressing

This is a simple but very tasty basic salad in a light mayonnaise-style dressing.

Ingredients for 2

350g/12oz new potatoes
2 tbsp good mayonnaise
2 tbsp natural yoghurt
½ red onion, finely chopped
1 tbsp snipped fresh chives
salt and freshly ground black pepper

Ingredients for 4

700g/1½lb new potatoes
4 tbsp good mayonnaise
4 tbsp natural yoghurt
1 red onion, finely chopped
2 tbsp snipped fresh chives
salt and freshly ground black pepper

3

1 Peel or scrub the potatoes. Place in a saucepan with just enough water to cover.

2 Bring to the boil over a high heat, then reduce the heat and cook for 12–15 minutes until just tender. Drain.

3 Cool slightly. Peel if desired, then cut into bite-size pieces.

4

4 Combine the mayonnaise and yoghurt in a small bowl. Stir in the onion and chives. Season with salt and pepper.

5 Pour over the potatoes and toss gently to combine.

6 Serve at room temperature or lightly chilled.

5

Gnocchi with Fresh Tomato Sauce

Made from humble ingredients yet very filling; economical and tasty too.

Ingredients for 2	Ingredients for 4
Gnocchi:	**Gnocchi:**
250g/9oz floury potatoes	500g/1lb 2oz floury potatoes
50g/2oz plain flour	100g/4oz plain flour
1 egg yolk	2 egg yolks
a few fresh basil leaves	a small handful basil leaves
Sauce:	**Sauce:**
1 tbsp extra virgin oil	2 tbsp extra virgin oil
1/2 small onion, chopped	1 small onion, chopped
225g/8oz tomatoes, seeded and chopped	450g/1lb tomatoes, seeded and chopped
salt and freshly ground black pepper	salt and freshly ground black pepper

1 Cook the potatoes in their skins in a pan of lightly salted boiling water until just tender. Drain and cool under running water. Drain again.

2 Peel the potatoes and mash well. Add the flour and egg yolks. Chop the basil and add to the bowl. Season well. Beat until well combined to form a soft dough.

3 Working on a floured surface, take pieces of the dough and roll into a rope about 1cm/1/2in thick. Cut into pieces about 2cm/1in long. Roll each piece over the tines of a fork to mark. Set aside while preparing the sauce.

4 Heat the oil in a saucepan and sauté the onion for 5 minutes until softened. Add the tomatoes and cook gently for 10 minutes. Season.

5 To cook the gnocchi bring a large saucepan of water to the boil. Add the gnocchi and simmer until they float to the top. Remove with a draining spoon and transfer to a warm serving dish. Spoon the tomato sauce on top.

2

3

5

Bacon Rösti with Creamy Mushrooms

The creamy mushrooms served with the rösti could also be tossed with plain boiled new potatoes. Choose a mixture of mushrooms, such as button, chestnut and oyster mushrooms.

1 To prepare the rösti, heat the oil in a large frying pan and fry the onion and bacon for 5–8 minutes until the onion is softened and just beginning to colour. Allow to cool.

2 Coarsely grate the potato and place in a sieve. Put a saucer or small plate on top and press down, squeezing out as much liquid as you can.

3 Add the bacon mixture to the grated potatoes. Sprinkle over the flour and then add the egg. Season and mix well.

4 Slice the mushrooms. Heat the oil in a small pan and fry for 3–4 minutes until tender.

5 Add the cream cheese and milk and cook gently, stirring until the cheese melts and forms a sauce. Keep warm.

6 Heat a large heavy-based pan or flat griddle and lightly oil the surface. Divide the potato mixture into 2 (4). Spoon one portion into the pan and spread to form a circle. Cook until the underside is dark golden and crisp.

7 Flip over and cook the other side. Allow about 3 minutes each side. Drain in kitchen paper and keep warm while cooking the remainder.

8 Serve the rösti topped with the creamy mushrooms.

1

3

5

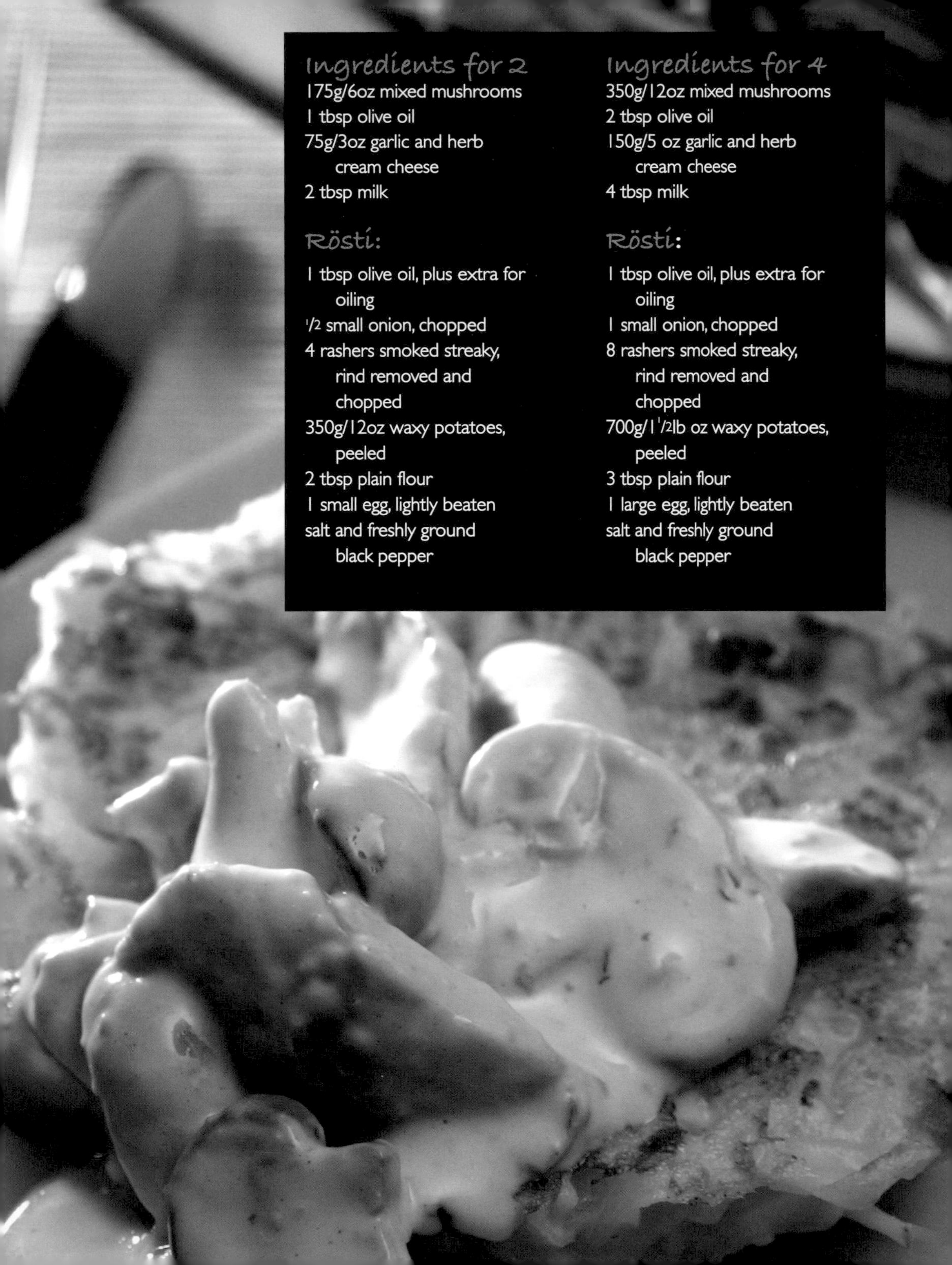

Ingredients for 2

175g/6oz mixed mushrooms
1 tbsp olive oil
75g/3oz garlic and herb cream cheese
2 tbsp milk

Rösti:

1 tbsp olive oil, plus extra for oiling
½ small onion, chopped
4 rashers smoked streaky, rind removed and chopped
350g/12oz waxy potatoes, peeled
2 tbsp plain flour
1 small egg, lightly beaten
salt and freshly ground black pepper

Ingredients for 4

350g/12oz mixed mushrooms
2 tbsp olive oil
150g/5 oz garlic and herb cream cheese
4 tbsp milk

Rösti:

1 tbsp olive oil, plus extra for oiling
1 small onion, chopped
8 rashers smoked streaky, rind removed and chopped
700g/1½lb oz waxy potatoes, peeled
3 tbsp plain flour
1 large egg, lightly beaten
salt and freshly ground black pepper

Bubble and Squeak

Great for using leftover potato or cabbage, but delicious enough to make from scratch. Although bubble and squeak can be used as a side dish I think it makes a great midweek meal in itself, especially if served with bacon and grilled tomatoes.

Ingredients for 2

500g/1lb 2oz floury potatoes, peeled
100–175g/4–6oz cabbage or spring greens
25g/1oz butter
1 tbsp sunflower oil
salt and freshly ground black pepper

Ingredients for 4

900g/2lb floury potatoes, peeled
225g/8oz cabbage or spring greens
40g/1½oz butter
2 tbsp sunflower oil
salt and freshly ground black pepper

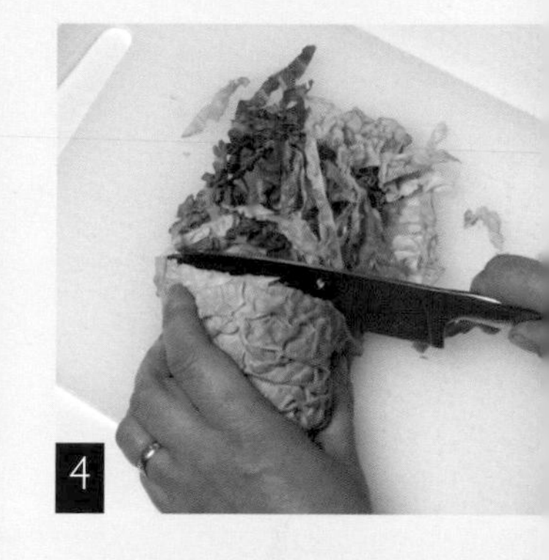
4

1 Cut the potatoes into large dice.

2 Bring a pan of lightly salted water to the boil. Add the potatoes and return to the boil. Simmer for 5–8 minutes until tender.

3 Drain and mash well

4 Meanwhile, shred the cabbage and cook in another pan of boiling water for 4–5 minutes until tender. Drain well.

5 Heat the butter and oil in a heavy-based frying pan. Add the potato and cabbage and mix together. Season with salt and pepper.

5

6 Spread out in a layer in the pan and cook for 2–3 minutes until a crust forms on the base.

7 Break up the mixture, then press down into the pan and cook for a further 1–2 minutes.

8 Repeat this once or twice more so that the bubble and squeak is piping hot and there are bits of golden, crispy potato crust in the mixture. Serve immediately.

7

Baked Potatoes with Mediterranean Roast Vegetables

Fluffy potato in a crispy shell topped with roasted vegetables makes a perfect combination.

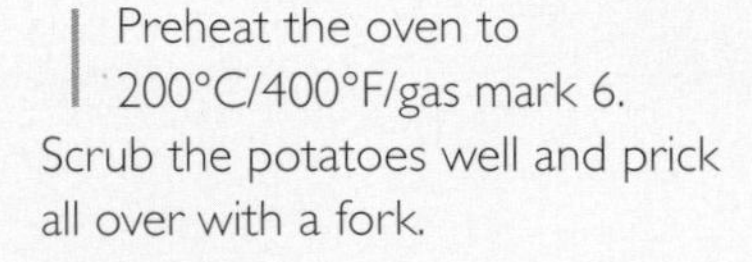

1 Preheat the oven to 200°C/400°F/gas mark 6. Scrub the potatoes well and prick all over with a fork.

2 Place on a baking sheet and bake near the top of the oven for 1½ hours, turning once.

3 Spread the prepared vegetables and garlic in a roasting tin. Sprinkle with olive oil and rosemary. Season with salt and pepper.

4 Roast the vegetables below the potatoes for 45–50 minutes until soft and beginning to char at the edges.

5 When cooked, cut a large cross into the potatoes and gently open.

6 Divide the cheese between the potatoes.

7 Place on a serving plate and serve topped with the roasted vegetables.

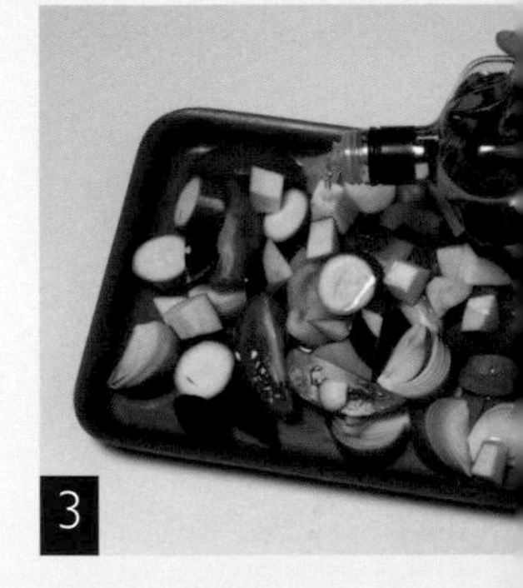

Ingredients for 2

- 2 baking potatoes about 275g/10oz each
- 1/4 small aubergine, cut into chunks
- 1 small courgette, cut into thick slices
- 1/2 red onion, cut into wedges
- 1/2 red pepper, seeded and cut into chunks
- 1/2 yellow pepper, seeded and cut into chunks
- 1 plum tomato, quartered
- 1 clove garlic, sliced
- 1 tbsp olive oil
- 1 tsp chopped fresh rosemary
- 50g/2oz mozzarella cheese, cut into cubes
- salt and freshly ground black pepper

Ingredients for 4

- 4 baking potatoes about 275g/10oz each
- 1/2 small aubergine, cut into chunks
- 1 courgette, cut into thick slices
- 1 red onion, cut into wedges
- 1 red pepper, seeded and cut into chunks
- 1 yellow pepper, seeded and cut into chunks
- 2 plum tomatoes, quartered
- 1 clove garlic, sliced
- 2 tbsp olive oil
- 1 tbsp chopped fresh rosemary
- 100g/4oz mozzarella cheese, cut into cubes
- salt and freshly ground black pepper

Spicy Oven Chips with Onion Wedges

Liven up everyday meals with these spicy oven-baked chips.

Ingredients for 2

350g/12oz potatoes
1 red onion
2 cloves garlic, peeled and halved
1 tbsp lemon juice
1 tbsp water
2 tsp tomato purée
2 tbsp olive oil
1/2 tsp dried mixed herbs
1 tsp paprika
1/2 tsp chilli powder
salt and freshly ground black pepper

Ingredients for 4

700g/1 1/2lb potatoes
2 red onions
4 cloves garlic, peeled and halved
2 tbsp lemon juice
2 tbsp water
1 tbsp tomato purée
4 tbsp olive oil
1 tsp dried mixed herbs
2 tsp paprika
1 tsp chilli powder
salt and freshly ground black pepper

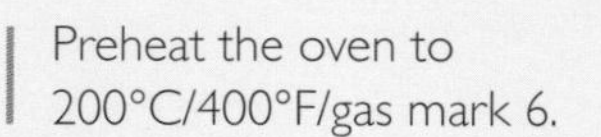

1 Preheat the oven to 200°C/400°F/gas mark 6.

2 Peel and cut the potatoes into chunky chips.

3 Peel the onions and cut into wedges.

4 Toss the potato chips, garlic and onion together in a large bowl.

5 Place the lemon juice, water, tomato purée and oil in a small bowl and whisk together with a fork.

6 Stir in the herbs and spices. Drizzle over the potato and onion mixture and toss together to coat well. Season with salt and pepper.

7 Spread out in a single layer on a baking sheet.

8 Bake for 40–50 minutes until the potatoes are tender.

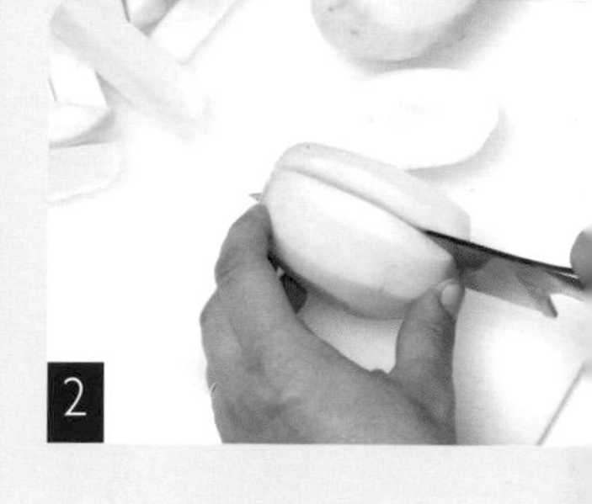

Chunky Herbed Oven Chips

With much less fat than fried chips these chips can become a regular treat. I love the crunch of the flakes of Maldon salt on chips. There is no need to grind the salt, just sprinkle a little over the chips.

Ingredients for 2

250g/9oz medium floury potatoes, cut into wedges
2 tbsp olive oil
1/4 tsp dried rosemary
1/4 tsp dried thyme
generous pinch dried sage
sea salt, preferably Maldon

Ingredients for 4

500g/1lb 2oz medium floury potatoes, cut into wedges
3 tbsp olive oil
1/2 tsp dried rosemary
1/2 tsp dried thyme
1/4 tsp dried sage
sea salt, preferably Maldon

2

1 Preheat the oven to 200°C/400°F/gas mark 6.

2 Place the potatoes in a bowl of water for 10 minutes to remove excess starch. Drain well and pat dry with kitchen paper or a clean tea towel.

3 Put the potatoes, oil and herbs in a large bowl and toss together until well coated.

4 Spread out on a baking sheet in a single layer.

5 Bake in the centre of the oven for 30–40 minutes, turning once or twice to ensure even browning.

6 When tender and golden, sprinkle with salt and serve immediately.

3

4

Crushed Roast Potatoes with Olive and Sun-dried Tomato Dressing

Tossed in a piquant dressing, these potatoes are fabulous served with barbecued or plain grilled meat and fish. Crushing the potatoes means that some of the flavour is absorbed into the potato itself.

Ingredients for 2

450g/1lb baby new potatoes
4 tbsp extra virgin olive oil
1/2 red onion, roughly chopped
4 sun-dried tomatoes
4 pitted black olives, chopped
a small handful flat-leaved parsley
1 tbsp red wine vinegar
salt and freshly ground black pepper

Ingredients for 4

900g/2lb baby new potatoes
6 tbsp extra virgin olive oil
1 small red onion, roughly chopped
8 sun-dried tomatoes
8 pitted black olives, chopped
a large handful flat-leaved parsley
2 tbsp red wine vinegar
salt and freshly ground black pepper

1 Preheat the oven to 200°C/400°F/gas mark 6.

2 Place the potatoes in a roasting tin and drizzle with 2 tbsp (3 tbsp) of the oil.

3 Sprinkle with a little salt and roast for 30 minutes, turning occasionally until tender.

4 Meanwhile, place the remaining oil, onion, tomatoes, olives, parsley and vinegar in a food processor and chop finely.

5 Lightly crush each potato with a fork and then toss in the onion and parsley mixture. Serve immediately.

3

4

5

Orange-glazed New Potatoes

A simple glaze gives new potatoes a tasty twist.

Ingredients for 2	Ingredients for 4
350g/12oz small new potatoes	700g/1 1/2lb small new potatoes
15g/1/2oz butter	25g/1oz butter
1/2 tsp grated orange zest	1 tsp grated orange zest
2 tbsp orange juice	4 tbsp orange juice
1 tbsp light muscovado sugar	2 tbsp light muscovado sugar
1/4 tsp ground cumin	1/2 tsp ground cumin
about 4 basil leaves, shredded	about 4 basil leaves, shredded
salt and freshly ground black pepper	salt and freshly ground black pepper
basil leaves to garnish	basil leaves to garnish

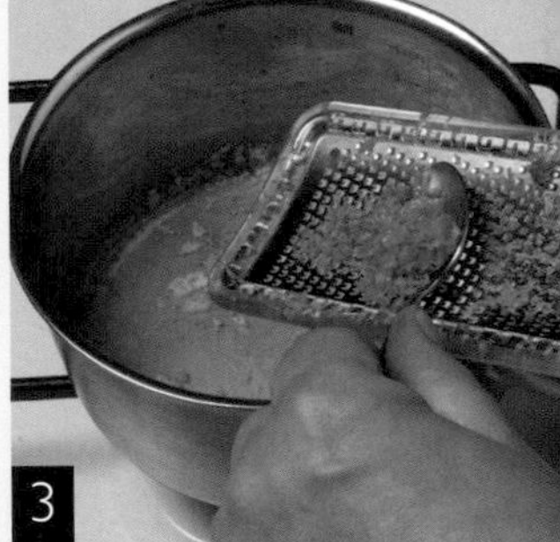

1 Place the potatoes in a saucepan with just enough water to cover. Bring to the boil, reduce heat, cover and simmer for 15–20 minutes until tender.

2 Drain, return to the pan and keep warm.

3 Melt the butter in a small pan and stir in the orange zest, juice, sugar and cumin.

4 Pour the orange glaze over the potatoes. Add the shredded basil and toss to coat well. Pile into a serving dish and serve garnished with basil leaves.

New Potatoes with Minted Peas and Pancetta

Serve this dish with plain grilled meat or chicken for a complete meal.

Ingredients for 2

- 250g/9oz baby new potatoes, washed
- 175g/6oz frozen peas
- 1 tbsp olive oil
- 50g/2oz diced pancetta
- 4 spring onions, sliced
- 4 tbsp reduced-fat crème fraîche
- 1 tbsp chopped fresh mint
- salt and freshly ground black pepper
- fresh mint to garnish

Ingredients for 4

- 500g/1lb 2oz baby new potatoes washed
- 350g/12oz frozen peas
- 2 tbsp olive oil
- 100g/4oz diced pancetta
- 8 spring onions, sliced
- 125g/4½oz reduced-fat crème fraîche
- 2 tbsp chopped fresh mint
- salt and freshly ground black pepper
- fresh mint to garnish

1

2

3

1 Bring a large saucepan of water to the boil and add the potatoes. Bring the water back to boiling over a high heat and simmer for 12 minutes until the potatoes are almost tender.

2 Add the peas and return to the boil to simmer for 2–3 minutes.

3 Meanwhile, heat the olive oil in a frying pan and sauté the pancetta until beginning to brown. Add the spring onions and sauté until just softened.

4 Stir in the crème fraîche and mint.

5 When the potatoes and peas are cooked, drain and add to the frying pan.

6 Toss until coated in the sauce, season to taste and garnish with mint. Serve immediately.

New Potatoes with Gremolata

Cooked in paper parcels with fresh herbs and the delicious tang of lemons, this potato dish is full of flavour. Greaseproof paper can also be used but it is not as strong as baking parchment so use double thickness.

2

Ingredients for 2

450g/1lb baby new potatoes
2 tbsp chopped fresh parsley
2 tbsp chopped fresh mint
1 tsp lemon zest
1 tsp capers, rinsed and chopped
1 tsp lemon juice
2 tbsp extra virgin olive oil
salt and freshly ground black pepper

Ingredients for 4

900g/2lb baby new potatoes
4 tbsp chopped fresh parsley
4 tbsp chopped fresh mint
1 tbsp lemon zest
1 tbsp capers, rinsed and chopped
1 tbsp lemon juice
4 tbsp extra virgin olive oil
salt and freshly ground black pepper

3

1 Preheat the oven to 190°C/375°F/gas mark 5. Wash the potatoes and divide them equally between 2 (4) large squares of non-stick baking parchment.

2 Combine all the remaining ingredients.

3 Spoon equally over the potatoes.

4 Fold up the paper to form parcels that completely enclose the potatoes.

5 Place on a baking sheet and bake for 40–45 minutes, or until the potatoes are tender. Serve in the paper.

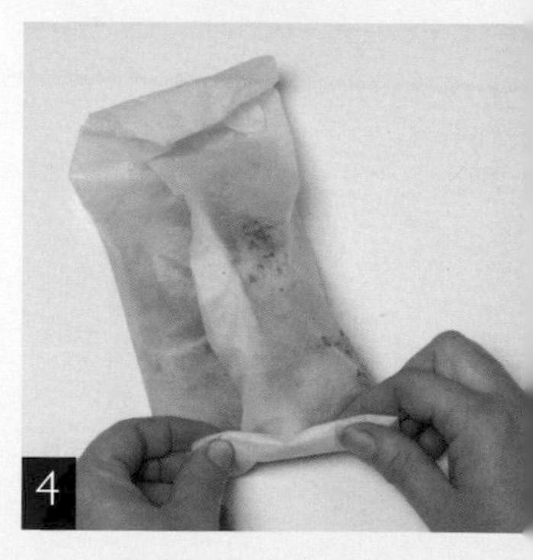
4

Saag Aloo

This is a favourite of mine, which I have to order whenever I go to an Indian restaurant. It is also very easy to make at home, so my potato cookbook would not be complete without it.

Ingredients for 2

- 1/4 tsp cumin seeds
- 1/4 tsp fennel seeds
- 1/4 tsp coriander seeds
- 2 tbsp ghee or sunflower oil
- 1 small onion, chopped
- 1 tbsp fresh ginger, chopped
- 1/2 green chilli, seeded if desired and chopped
- 1/4 tsp salt
- 1/2 tsp ground turmeric
- 2 tsp lemon juice
- about 75ml/2 1/2fl oz water
- 450g/1lb floury potatoes, peeled and cut into chunks
- 225g/8oz spinach, washed

Ingredients for 4

- 1/2 tsp cumin seeds
- 1/2 tsp fennel seeds
- 1/2 tsp coriander seeds
- 4 tbsp ghee or sunflower oil
- 1 onion, chopped
- 2 tbsp fresh ginger, chopped
- 1 green chilli, seeded if desired and chopped
- 1/2 tsp salt
- 1 tsp ground turmeric
- 1 tbsp lemon juice
- about 150ml/1/4pt water
- 900g/2lb small floury potatoes, peeled and cut into chunks
- 450g/1lb spinach, washed

1

2

4

1 Heat the seeds in a dry frying pan until they begin to pop. Pour into a pestle and mortar and grind coarsely.

2 Heat the ghee or oil in a large saucepan and add the onion, ginger and chilli. Fry for 3–4 minutes until the onion begins to soften.

3 Add the ground seeds, salt, turmeric and lemon juice. Stir in the potatoes and water. Bring to the boil, reduce the heat, cover and cook over a low heat for about 10 minutes until the potatoes are almost tender.

4 Stir in the spinach and cook for a further 5 minutes, until the spinach has wilted and the potatoes are completely tender. Stir frequently to prevent it burning on the bottom of the pan. The mixture should be quite dry.

Caramelised Potatoes

The caramel coating can be used on other root vegetables such as carrots, turnips or parsnips, but I prefer it most with potatoes.

Ingredients for 2

450g/1lb small potatoes, peeled
25g/1oz butter
25g/1oz light muscovado sugar
1 tbsp water
salt
chopped fresh parsley to garnish

Ingredients for 4

900g/2lb small potatoes, peeled
50g/2oz butter
50g/2oz light muscovado sugar
2 tbsp water
salt
chopped fresh parsley to garnish

2

3

4

1 Bring a pan of water to the boil and lightly salt. Add the potatoes and simmer for 12–15 minutes until almost tender. Drain.

2 Heat the butter in a sauté pan and stir in the sugar. Stir until the sugar dissolves then boil until slightly syrupy. Take care not to let the mixture burn; it should be a golden brown colour.

3 Add the water, taking care as it may splutter.

4 Swirl the pan and add the potatoes. Cook gently for about 10 minutes, shaking the pan occasionally, until the potatoes are golden and tender when pierced with a skewer.

5 Transfer to a warm serving dish and allow to stand for 2–3 minutes before serving.

Shepherd's Pie

A classic all-time family favourite.

1 Heat the oil in a large saucepan and fry the onion and garlic until softened.

2 Add the mince and cook, breaking up the mince with the side of a spoon, until browned.

3 Stir in the herbs and flour.

4 Gradually add the stock and Worcestershire sauce, stirring until thickened slightly. Reduce heat and simmer while preparing the topping.

5 Heat the oven to 190°C/375°F/gas mark 5.

6 Cook the potatoes in lightly salted boiling water for 12–15 minutes until tender.

7 Drain and return to the pan. Add the milk and butter and season. Mash well.

8 Season the meat to taste and pour into an ovenproof baking dish. Spoon off any excess fat.

9 Carefully spread the mashed potato on top of the mince, fluffing it with a fork.

10 Sprinkle the cheese over the top, if using. Bake for 25 minutes, or until the potato is crisp and golden.

2

3

9

Ingredients for 2

- 2 tsp sunflower oil
- 1 small onion, chopped
- 1 clove garlic, chopped
- 250g/9oz lean minced lamb
- ½ tsp dried mixed herbs
- 2 tsp plain flour
- 150ml/¼pt lamb or vegetable stock
- 2 tsp Worcestershire sauce
- 450g/1lb floury potatoes, peeled and cut into chunks
- splash milk
- knob butter
- 40g/1½oz Cheddar cheese (optional)
- salt and freshly ground black pepper

Ingredients for 4

- 1 tbsp sunflower oil
- 1 large onion, chopped
- 1 clove garlic, chopped
- 500g/1lb 2oz lean minced lamb
- 1 tsp dried mixed herbs
- 1 tbsp plain flour
- 300ml/½pt lamb or vegetable stock
- 1 tbsp Worcestershire sauce
- 900g/2lb floury potatoes, peeled and cut into chunks
- 4 tbsp milk
- 25g/1oz butter
- 50g/2oz Cheddar cheese (optional)
- salt and freshly ground black pepper

Spring Lamb Casserole

Cooked in the casserole the potatoes absorb the flavour of the meat, making this a delicious meal in one.

Ingredients for 2

- 1 tbsp sunflower oil
- 4 lean lamb chops
- 225g/8oz new carrots, scraped and cut in half if large
- 250g/8oz baby new potatoes
- 300ml/½pt vegetable or lamb stock
- 1 sprig fresh thyme
- 1 sprig rosemary
- bay leaf
- 100g/4oz shelled broad beans
- salt and freshly ground black pepper
- chopped fresh parsley, to garnish (optional)

Ingredients for 4

- 2 tbsp sunflower oil
- 8 lean lamb chops
- 450g/1lb new carrots, scraped and cut in half if large
- 500g/1lb 2oz baby new potatoes
- 600ml/1pt vegetable or lamb stock
- 2 sprigs fresh thyme
- 2 sprigs rosemary
- bay leaf
- 225g/8oz shelled broad beans
- salt and freshly ground black pepper
- chopped fresh parsley, to garnish (optional)

1 Heat the oil in a heavy-based pan and fry the meat until browned on both sides.

2 Add the carrots and potatoes and toss well. Stir in the stock and herbs. Season with salt and pepper.

3 Bring gently to the boil, cover and simmer gently for 45 minutes.

4 Add the broad beans. Continue to cook for 20 minutes until the lamb is done and all the vegetables are tender.

5 Remove herb sprigs and sprinkle with chopped parsley to serve, if desired.

Beer and Beef Hotpot

A warming winter meal that is perfect for colder days. Just add a fresh green vegetable for a complete meal.

Ingredients for 2

- 1 tbsp sunflower oil, plus extra for brushing
- 1 onion, sliced
- 250g/9oz lean braising steak, cut into cubes
- 15g/½oz plain flour
- 150ml/¼pt brown ale
- 175ml/6fl oz beef stock
- ¼ tsp caster sugar
- 100g/4oz mushrooms, sliced
- 100g/4oz carrots, sliced
- 500g/1lb 2oz potatoes, peeled
- salt and freshly ground black pepper

Ingredients for 4

- 2 tbsp sunflower oil, plus extra for brushing
- 1 large onion, sliced
- 500g/1lb 2oz lean braising steak, cut into cubes
- 25g/1oz plain flour
- 300ml/½pt brown ale
- 450ml/¾pt beef stock
- ½ tsp caster sugar
- 225g/8oz mushrooms, sliced
- 225g/8oz carrots, sliced
- 1kg/2¼lb potatoes, peeled
- salt and freshly ground black pepper

1 Heat the oil in a large pan and gently fry the onion until it begins to soften. Add the meat and cook until browned on all sides.

2 Sprinkle the flour into the pan and cook for a few seconds. Stir in the ale and stock and bring to the boil, stirring. Add the sugar. Simmer for 30 minutes.

3 Preheat the oven to 170°C/325°F/gas mark 3.

4 Stir in the mushrooms and carrots. Season with salt and pepper. Thickly slice the potatoes. Place a layer of potatoes in the bottom of a deep ovenproof casserole. Spoon some of the meat mixture over the potatoes. Repeat layers, finishing with a layer of potatoes.

5 Brush the top of the potatoes with a little oil. Cover with foil and bake for 1 hour. Remove the foil and bake for a further 30 minutes, or until the meat is tender and the potatoes are golden.

Roast Lamb with Potatoes Boulangere

This classic French dish gets its name from the days when the Sunday roast was taken to the local baker to be cooked in his ovens. You can place the lamb directly on the potatoes but I prefer to place it directly on the oven shelf above. The juices will still drop into the potatoes but in this way you get the maximum amount of crispy potatoes on the top, which I love.

Ingredients for 4 to 6

½ leg lamb about 1 kg/2¼lb in weight
1 clove garlic, sliced
1 onion, thinly sliced
700g/1½lb waxy potatoes
salt and white pepper
¼ tsp dried thyme
150ml/¼pt hot beef, chicken or vegetable stock
25g/1oz butter

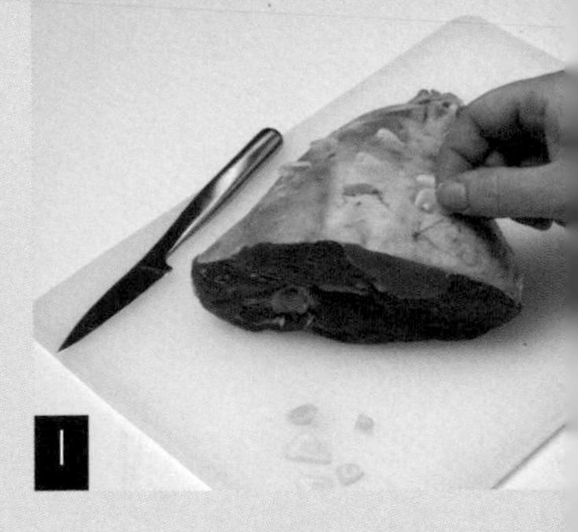

1

1 Preheat the oven to 190°C/375°F/gas mark 5. Use a sharp knife to cut small slits into the surface of the lamb. Push a slice of garlic into each.

2 Peel and thinly slice the potatoes, ideally with a mandolin or the slicing attachment of a food processor. Rinse and pat dry.

3 Lightly grease a shallow baking dish and place a layer of potatoes in it. Place a layer of onions on top. Repeat the layers, finishing with a layer of potato. Season each layer with salt, pepper and a little of the thyme.

3

4 Pour the stock over the potatoes and dot the top with butter. Place in the oven with the lamb directly on the shelf above, so that the juices of the lamb will drop onto the potatoes.

5 Roast the lamb for 1¼ hours and the potatoes for 1½ hours. Leave the lamb in a warm place while the potatoes finish cooking, about 15 minutes.

4

Sausages with Onion Gravy and Celeriac Mash

Comfort food at its best. The addition of celeriac to the mash gives a more sophisticated flavour, making this dish ideal for informal entertaining.

2

1 Heat the butter and oil in a saucepan and fry the onions over a low heat for 10 minutes until very soft.

2 Stir in the sugar and flour. Gradually add the Madeira or wine and then stir in the stock.

3 Bring to the boil, reduce the heat and simmer for 15 minutes.

4 Fry or grill the sausages for 15–20 minutes, turning frequently.

5 Meanwhile, peel and cut the potato and celeriac into 2.5cm/1in chunks. Cook them in lightly salted boiling water for 10–12 minutes, or until just tender.

6 Drain well. Add the butter and milk and mash well. Season to taste.

7 Serve the mash with the sausages and onion gravy.

4

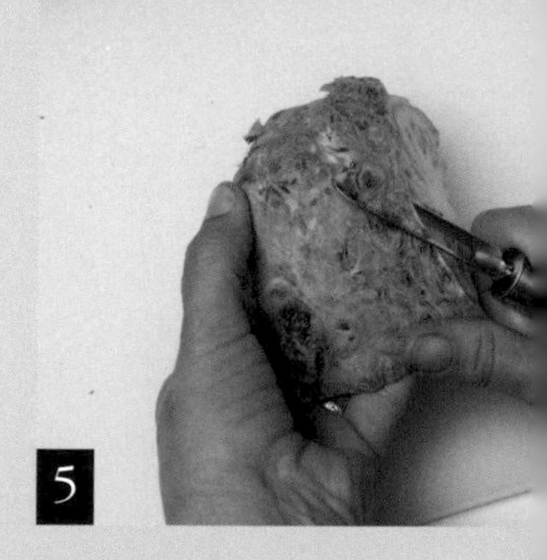
5

Ingredients for 2

15g/½oz butter
2 tsp olive oil
1 large onion, sliced
pinch dark brown sugar
1 tbsp plain flour
3 tbsp Madeira or red wine
150ml/¼pt good vegetable or beef stock
4 good-quality pork sausages

Celeriac Mash

225g/8oz floury potatoes
225g/8oz celeriac
25g/1oz butter
splash of milk
salt and freshly ground black pepper

Ingredients for 4

25g/1oz butter
1 tbsp olive oil
2 large onions, sliced
¼ tsp dark brown sugar
2 tbsp plain flour
100ml/3½fl oz Madeira or red wine
300ml/½pt good vegetable or beef stock
8 good-quality pork sausages

Celeriac Mash

450g/1lb floury potatoes
450g/1lb celeriac
50g/2oz butter
4 tbsp milk
salt and freshly ground black pepper

Fish Pie

This variation of a classic dish has a tasty topping of crunchy cubed potatoes rather than the more familiar mash. It is ideal for a midweek meal.

Ingredients for 2

- 175g/6oz cod or haddock fillet, skinned
- 175g/6oz smoked haddock fillet, skinned
- 300ml/½pt milk
- 40g/1½oz butter
- 1 leek, washed and sliced
- 25g/1oz plain flour
- 1 hard-boiled egg, cut into quarters
- 450g/1lb potatoes, peeled and cut into 1cm/½in cubes
- salt and freshly ground black pepper

Ingredients for 4

- 350g/12oz cod or haddock fillet, skinned
- 350g/12oz smoked haddock fillet, skinned
- 600ml/1pt milk
- 75g/3oz butter
- 2 leeks, washed and sliced
- 50g/2oz plain flour
- 2 hard-boiled eggs, cut into quarters
- 900g/2lb potatoes, peeled and cut into 1cm/½in cubes
- salt and freshly ground black pepper

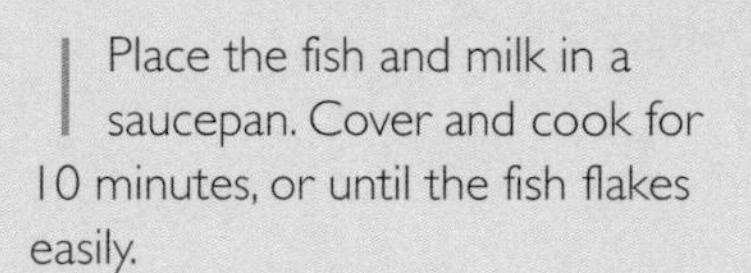

1 Place the fish and milk in a saucepan. Cover and cook for 10 minutes, or until the fish flakes easily.

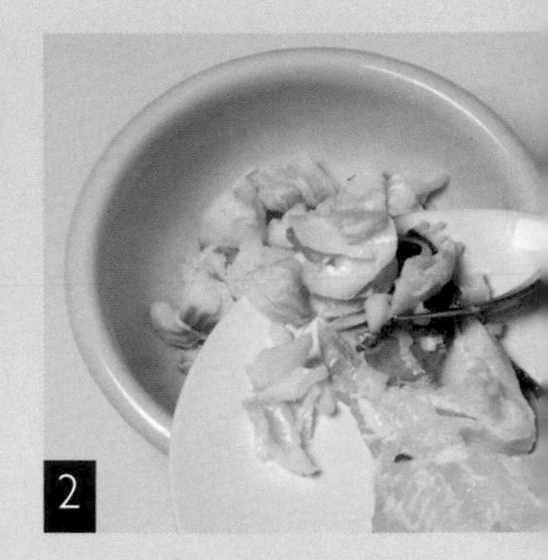

2

2 Remove the fish with a draining spoon. Strain the milk through a sieve and reserve. Flake the fish in large chunks.

3 Melt 25g/1oz (50g/2oz) butter in a saucepan and add the leek. Cook gently for 3 minutes, or until softened. Stir in the flour and cook for another minute.

4

4 Gradually stir in the milk and cook, stirring constantly, until the sauce thickens. Season to taste with salt and pepper.

5

5 Place the fish in an ovenproof dish and arrange the egg on top. Spoon the sauce over the fish.

6 Cook the potatoes in lightly salted boiling water for 5 minutes. Drain. Arrange on top of the egg.

7 Melt the remaining butter and brush over the top. Bake for 35–45 minutes at 200°C/400°F/gas mark 6 until the top is crisp and golden.

Perfect Fish and Chip Supper

The key to good fish and chips is ensuring that the oil is at the correct temperature and that you do not crowd the pan too much.

Ingredients for 2	Ingredients for 4
2 x 175g/6oz fillets of cod or haddock	4 x 175g/6oz fillets of cod or haddock
100g/3½fl oz plain flour	200g/7oz plain flour
1 tsp baking powder	1 tsp baking powder
½ tsp malt vinegar	1 tsp malt vinegar
about 100ml/4fl oz water	about 200ml/7fl oz water
500g/1lb 2oz potatoes	1kg/2lb 4oz potatoes
oil for deep-frying	oil for deep-frying
salt and freshly ground black pepper	salt and freshly ground black pepper

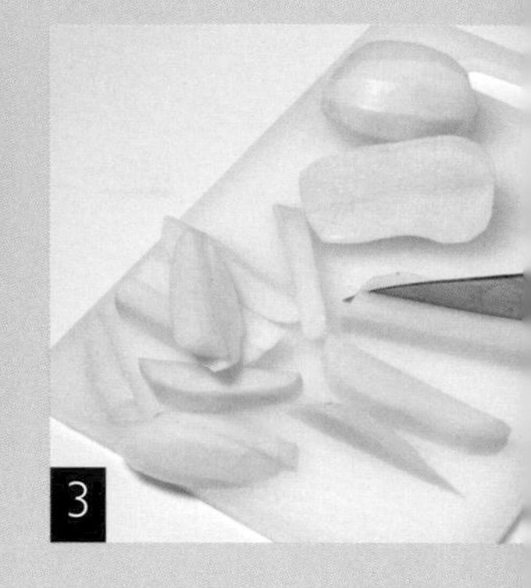
3

1 Skin the fish, if desired, and season with salt and pepper.

2 Make the batter by placing the flour and baking powder in a small bowl and making a well in the centre. Add the vinegar and gradually whisk in enough water to form a smooth, thick batter.

3 Peel and cut the potatoes into 1cm/½in thick chips.

4 Heat the oil in a deep-fat fryer or large saucepan to 180°C/350°F. (If using a saucepan do not fill more than one-third full.)

5 Add the chips and blanch for 5 minutes until just tender. You will need to do this in two batches if you are cooking for four people. Drain on kitchen paper and set aside.

6

6 Allow the temperature of the oil to come to 180–185°C/350–360°F. It may have dropped below this. Dip the fish into the batter and shake off excess.

7 Deep-fry the fish for 5–6 minutes until crisp and golden. Drain on kitchen paper and transfer to a warm serving plate. Keep warm.

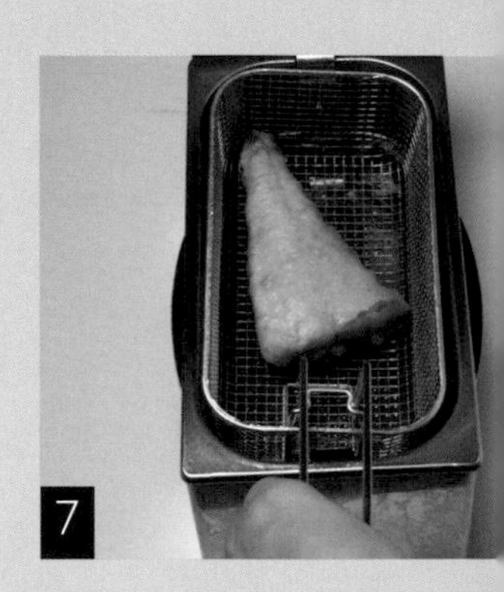
7

8 Heat the oil again, this time to 190°C/375°F. Return the chips for 2–3 minutes until crisp and golden and piping hot. Again this is best done in two batches, if cooking for four people, to prevent the temperature of the oil dropping too much.

9 Drain well and serve with the fish.

Mixed Root Mash

This dish has been a favourite of mine since the children were toddlers. It has a slightly sweet flavour that is popular with children.

Ingredients for 2

200g/7oz floury potatoes, peeled
100g/4oz sweet potatoes, peeled
100g/4oz parsnips, peeled
1 small carrot, peeled
2 tbsp olive oil
salt and freshly ground black pepper

Ingredients for 4

400g/14oz floury potatoes, peeled
200g/7oz sweet potatoes, peeled
200g/7oz parsnips, peeled
1 large carrot, peeled
4 tbsp olive oil
salt and freshly ground black pepper

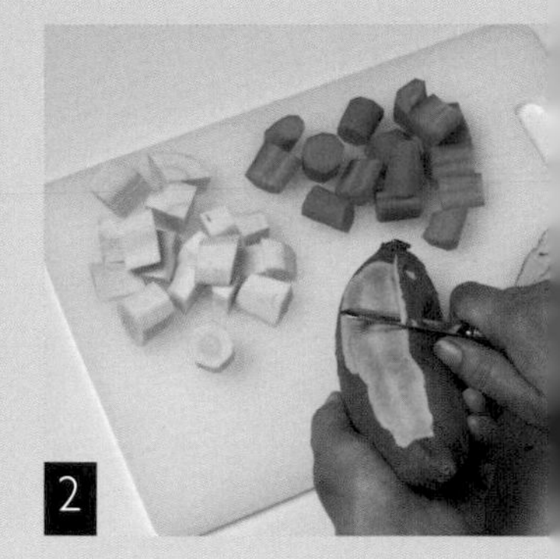
2

1 Cut the potatoes into small chunks. Place in a saucepan and add enough water to come about 2.5cm/1in above the potatoes. Bring quickly to the boil, add some salt, reduce the heat and simmer for 5 minutes.

2 Cut the other vegetables into small chunks.

3 Add to the pan and return to the boil, then cover and simmer for 5–6 minutes, or until all the vegetables are tender.

3

4 Drain, reserving a little of the cooking liquid. Add half the olive oil and mash until smooth. Beat in a few tablespoons of the cooking liquid. The mash should not be too wet and it should also have a mixture of textures, from the creamy potato to the chunky carrot and more fibrous parsnip.

5 Season with freshly ground black pepper. Pile the potato into a serving dish and drizzle over the remaining olive oil.

5

Potato Croquettes

Perfect for using leftover potato, these will be popular with young and old alike. I like the extra flavour the harissa paste gives the mash but it can be omitted, if preferred.

Ingredients for 2

350g/12oz cooked potatoes, mashed
4 spring onions, finely sliced
2 tsp harissa paste (optional)
2 tbsp chopped fresh parsley
1 small egg, beaten
40g/1½oz dried breadcrumbs
4 tbsp olive oil
salt and freshly ground black pepper
fresh parsley to garnish

Ingredients for 4

700g/1½lb cooked potatoes, mashed
bunch spring onions, finely sliced
1 tbsp harissa paste (optional)
4 tbsp chopped fresh parsley
1 egg, beaten
75g/3oz dried breadcrumbs
6 to 8 tbsp olive oil
salt and freshly ground black pepper
fresh parsley to garnish

2

3

4

1 Place the mashed potato in a bowl with the spring onion and harissa paste, if using.

2 Add the parsley, season to taste and mix well.

3 Divide into 4 (8) equal portions and shape into logs.

4 Dip each log in beaten egg and coat with breadcrumbs.

5 Heat the oil in a heavy-based frying pan and fry for 8–10 minutes, turning frequently until crisp and golden. Garnish with parsley.

Duchesse Potatoes

This classic dish is ideal when you need to prepare a dish in advance. Once made, it can be kept in the refrigerator and baked when required. I have given the dish a new twist with the addition of a little chilli and coriander, but you can leave the potato plain if you prefer. It is very important that the potato is smooth, or the piping will be difficult. Press through a nylon sieve if required. Freeze for up to 3 months. Cook from frozen, allowing an extra 5–10 minutes cooking time.

Ingredients for 2

350g/12oz floury potatoes
25g/1oz butter
1 small egg
1 tsp chilli purée
1 tbsp finely chopped coriander
beaten egg to glaze
salt

Ingredients for 4

700g/1½lb floury potatoes
50g/2oz butter
1 egg
2 tsp chilli purée
2 tbsp finely chopped coriander
beaten egg to glaze
salt

1 Peel the potatoes and cut into equal-size pieces. Place the potatoes in a saucepan and cover with water. Bring quickly to the boil, lightly salt the water, reduce the heat and simmer for 10–15 minutes, depending on the size of the pieces, until just tender.

2 Preheat the oven to 200°C/400°F/gas mark 6. Lightly grease one or two baking sheets.

3 Drain the potatoes and return the pan to the heat briefly to evaporate any liquid. Add the butter and mash until smooth.

4 Beat in the egg, chilli purée and coriander.

5 Pipe rosettes onto the prepared baking sheet. Add a splash of water to the beaten egg and carefully brush each rosette with beaten egg. Bake for 25 minutes until golden brown.

3

4

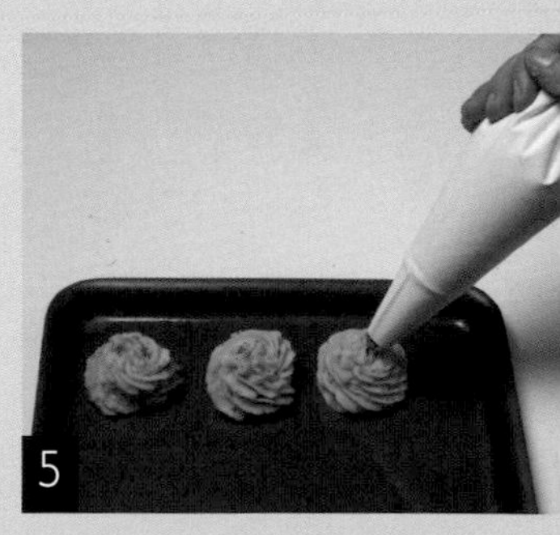
5

Perfect Roast Potatoes

Crisp on the outside, fluffy on the inside. Goose fat is my preferred fat for roast potatoes as it gives a crisp finish and a great flavour. You can buy it in delis and larger supermarkets. Choose medium-sized potatoes and cut into three or four pieces. Maris pipers are my favourite variety for roast potatoes.

Ingredients for 2

450g/1lb floury potatoes
4 tbsp goose fat, lard or sunflower oil
sea salt, preferably Maldon
coarsely ground black pepper

Ingredients for 4

900g/2lb floury potatoes
8 tbsp goose fat, lard or sunflower oil
sea salt, preferably Maldon
coarsely ground black pepper

5

6

7

1 Preheat the oven to 200°C/400°F/gas mark 6.

2 Peel and cut the potatoes so that all the pieces are about the same size.

3 Place in a saucepan of lightly salted water, cover and bring quickly to the boil.

4 Reduce the heat and simmer gently for 5 minutes.

5 Meanwhile, place the fat in a shallow-sided roasting tin and heat in the oven.

6 Drain the potatoes and return to the pan. Put the lid on the pan. Holding it in place, shake the pan up and down a few times. This will fluff up the outsides of the potatoes.

7 Tip the potatoes onto the tray and turn to coat in the hot fat.

8 Roast for 50–60 minutes, turning the potatoes once or twice during the cooking time. Serve immediately, sprinkled with salt and pepper.

Gratin Dauphinois

A classic French dish from the mountainous Dauphine region. There are two schools of thought: those who make the dish with the addition of grated cheese on top, and those who claim the true gratin Dauphinois does not contain cheese. So the choice is up to you!

Ingredients for 2

knob of butter
200ml/7fl oz double cream
75ml/2½fl oz milk
1 clove garlic, crushed
450g/1lb floury potatoes, peeled
25g/1oz Emmenthal cheese, grated (optional)
25g/1oz Gruyëre cheese grated (optional)
salt and freshly ground black pepper

Ingredients for 4

15g/½oz butter
400ml/14fl oz double cream
150ml/¼pt milk
2 cloves garlic, crushed
900g/2lb floury potatoes, peeled
50g/2oz Emmenthal cheese, grated (optional)
50g/2oz Gruyëre cheese, grated (optional)
salt and freshly ground black pepper

2

1 Preheat the oven to 170°C/325°F/gas mark 3. Generously grease a shallow, ovenproof dish with some of the butter.

2 Place the cream and milk in a saucepan with the garlic, and heat until just simmering. Remove from the heat. Season well with salt and pepper.

3

3 Thinly slice the potatoes and arrange in the dish, no more than six layers deep. Pour the cream mixture over the layers.

4 Mix together the cheeses, if using, and sprinkle over the top of the dish. Dot with any remaining butter.

5 Bake for about 1½ hours, or until the potatoes are tender and the top is golden.

4

INDEX

CREDITS & ACKNOWLEDGMENTS

This book is dedicated to the memory of my great aunt, Betty, a woman who liked nothing more than good plain cooking, preferably potato-based.

The Annual Register 1815 (biography of Antoine-Augustin Parmentier by Edmund Burke)
Beeton, Isabella *The Book of Household Management*
Glave, Luis Miguel, *The Potato, Treasure of the Andes*
From Agriculture to Culture: The Conquest of the Highlands, CIP Publications, 2001
Philips, Henry *History of Cultivated Vegetables*, 1822
Reader, John, *Propitious Esculent: The Potato in World History* Heinemann 2008
Romans, Alan *The Potato Book*, Frances Lincoln, 2005
Salaman, Redcliffe *The History and Social Influence of the Potato*, CUP, revised by W.G. Hoskins, 1985
Warrier, P.K. et al, *Indian Medicinal Plants: a compendium of 500 species*, Orient Longman, 1996
Zuckerman, Larry, *The Potato: The Story of How a Vegetable Changed History,* Pan Books, 2000

Websites
http://www.allotment.org.uk/vegetable/potato
http://www.allotment.org.uk/vegetable/potato
http://www.britishpotatoes.co.uk
http://www.cipotato.org
http://darwin-online.org.uk"http://darwin-online.org.uk
http://www.jbaseedpotatoes.co.uk
http://www.jerseyroyals.co.uk/
http://www.potato.com.au
http://www.potatomuseum.com
http://www.potato2008.org/en/index.html" http://www.potato2008.org
http://www.thompson-morgan.com
http://www.visionofbritain.org
http://whatscookingamerica.net

Picture credits
Images pp10, 17, 37, 54, 57, 58, 62 © Library of Congress
Images pp 13, 65, 125 © Idaho Potato Commission
Images pp 73, 74 bottom, 77 top, 78 bottom, 81, 82, 86, 89, 93, 94, 98, 101, 102 © Thompson & Morgan